P9-EKR-429

The

Big Book

of

Irony

ALSO BY JON WINOKUR

The
Big Book
of
Irony

Jon Winokur

St. Martin's Press
New York

www.stmartins.com

Design by Susan Walsh

Library of Congress Cataloging-in-Publication Data

Winokur, Jon.
    The big book of irony / Jon Winokur.—1st ed.
        p. cm.
    ISBN-13: 978-0-312-35483-1
    ISBN-10: 0-312-35483-5
    1. Irony. 2. Irony—Social aspects. 3. Irony in literature.

PN56.I65W56 2007
809'.918—dc22

                                                            2006051161

First Edition: February 2007

10 9 8 7 6 5 4 3 2 1

CONTENTS

i•ro•ny (ī′rə-nē, īər-)

n. pl. **i•ro•nies**

1.

a. The use of words to express something different from and often opposite to their literal meaning.

b. An expression or utterance marked by a deliberate contrast between apparent and intended meaning.

c. A literary style employing such contrasts for humorous or rhetorical effect. See synonyms at **wit**.

2.

a. Incongruity between what might be expected and what actually occurs:
"Hyde noted the irony of Ireland's copying the nation she most hated" (Richard Kain).

b. An occurence, result, or circumstance notable for such incongruity.

3. Dramatic irony.

4. Socratic irony.

The American Heritage Dictionary of the English Language, fourth edition

This world is a comedy to those that think, a tragedy to those that feel.

—Horace Walpole, *Letters* (1776)

INTRODUCTION

Irony is a protean phenomenon. It's a trope for saying one thing while meaning another or a way of looking at the world, a literary device or a pedagogical tool, a refuge for the witless or a secret handshake for the adept. Irony is an affectation for some, a genuine—even genetic—sensibility for others.

Lexicographers, critics, and philosophers don't agree on a definition. Ever since the ancient Greeks, they've been arguing over what irony is and how it works. (If the Greeks didn't invent irony, they gave it a name, *eirōnia,* for the artful pretense Socrates used to expose the ignorance of his opponents.) The noun (*yronye*) first appeared in the English language in 1502, the adjective (*ironick*) more than a century later (in Ben Jonson's play *The New Inn*). By 1755, Samuel Johnson's *Dictionary of the English Language* defined irony as "a mode of speech in which the meaning is clearly contrary to the words," with the example, "Bolingbroke is a holy man," implying that Johnson thought Bolingbroke a swine. Through the ages, skilled practitioners have used irony with powerful effect, from Jonathan

Swift's *A Modest Proposal* to the comedy of Sarah Silverman, from Jane Austen to Ali G, Shakespeare to Seinfeld.

Irony first attracted scholarly attention in 1841, when the Danish philosopher Søren Kierkegaard published *The Concept of Irony*, a recondite critique of "pure irony" as "infinite absolute negativity." Several landmark critical studies appeared in the twentieth century, most notably Wayne Booth's *A Rhetoric of Irony* in 1974, an elaborate analysis that declares appreciation of irony essential to intelligent reading. In 1996, Alanis Morissette's hit single "Ironic," in which situations purporting to be ironic are merely sad, random, or annoying (a traffic jam when you're running late, a no-smoking sign on your cigarette break) perpetuated misuse of the word and triggered debate over its meaning. Descriptivists, who see language as an evolving entity with the meanings of words ultimately determined by usage, excused Morissette's looseness. Prescriptivists countered that such linguistic drift is an agent of ignorance and took Morissette to task for the barbarism, gleefully noting the irony of an unironic song called "Ironic." In 1999, twenty-four-year-old Jedediah Purdy touched off a debate of irony's cultural significance with his book, *For Common Things: Irony, Trust, and Commitment in America Today*, an indictment of the "despairing irony" plaguing America. Purdy was lambasted by critics who, ironically, missed the point. Irony made news again after the attacks of 9/11, when commentators pronounced it dead. (The reports were exaggerated.)

Despite—or maybe because of—all the attention, irony is probably less understood now than ever. Much of the confusion comes from the existence of different forms of irony, the two most prominent of which are verbal irony—saying one thing but meaning another while intending to be understood as meaning the other—and what might be called ambient or cosmic irony, our perception of the vagaries of the human condition. Then there's dramatic irony, the effect achieved by allowing an audience to understand more than the characters; postmodern irony, a sardonic response to a dizzying age in which change is the only constant; auto-irony, whereby celebrities try to humanize themselves; and visual irony, in which an image contradicts itself, whether intentionally or not.

Irony has the uncanny ability to mirror itself: People misunderstand the meaning of the word *irony*; one of the meanings of the word *irony* is the misunderstanding of the meaning of words. Irony is a question that answers itself ("I *need* this?") or an answer that questions itself. (**Customer:** "Is the soup hot?" **Jewish waiter:** "No, it's cold.") Irony plies the gulf between appearance and reality, between what is and what ought to be, between what we hope for and what we get.

This book is an attempt to edify and entertain with irony's many facets. It's a small book, to be sure, but I hope the reader will agree that less is more.

J. W.
Pacific Palisades

NOTE ON BONUS IRONY

Little ironies tend to attach themselves to big ironies so that just when you think you've reaped all the irony from a given situation, another one crops up. Are these little irony supplements the result of some naturally occurring ironization process? More research is needed. Meantime, examples of such irony appearing throughout the book are labeled "bonus irony."

Toward
a Definition
of Irony

Irony is inherently confusing. Not only are its definitions confusing; it is confusing by definition.

—Jennifer Thompson, "Irony: A Few Simple Definitions,"
Teachers' Resource Web

Irony is the intentional transmission of both information and evaluative attitude other than what is explicitly presented.

—Linda Hutcheon, *Irony's Edge: The Theory and Politics of Irony* (1994)

Irony deals with opposites; it has nothing to do with coincidence. If two baseball players from the same hometown, on different teams, receive the same uniform number, it is not ironic. It is a coincidence. If Barry Bonds attains lifetime statistics identical to his father's, it will not be ironic. It will be a coincidence.

Irony is "a state of affairs that is the reverse of what

was to be expected; a result opposite to and in mockery of the appropriate result." For instance: A diabetic, on his way to buy insulin, is killed by a runaway truck. He is the victim of an accident. If the truck was delivering sugar, he is the victim of an oddly poetic coincidence. But if the truck was delivering insulin, ah! Then he is the victim of an irony.

If a Kurd, after surviving bloody battle with Saddam Hussein's army and a long, difficult escape through the mountains, is crushed and killed by a parachute drop of humanitarian aid, that, my friend, is irony writ large.

Darryl Stingley, the pro football player, was paralyzed after a brutal hit by Jack Tatum. Now Darryl Stingley's son plays football, and if the son should become paralyzed while playing, it will not be ironic. It will be coincidental. If Darryl Stingley's son paralyzes someone else, that will be closer to ironic. If he paralyzes Jack Tatum's son that will be precisely ironic.

—George Carlin, *Brain Droppings* (1997)

Irony is a way of containing two opposites in your head at the same time.

—Douglas Coupland, "The Post Modern Ironic Wink," *To the Best of Our Knowledge,* Wisconsin Public Radio, June 26, 2005

The word "irony" does not now mean only what it meant in earlier centuries, it does not mean in one country all it may mean in another, nor in the street what it may mean in the study, nor to one scholar what it may mean to another.

—D. C. Muecke, *Irony and the Ironic* (1982)

There are two broad uses in everyday parlance. The first relates to cosmic irony and has little to do with the play of language or figural speech. . . . This is an irony of situation, or an irony of existence; it is as though human life and its understanding of the world is undercut by some other meaning or design beyond our powers. . . . The word irony refers to the limits of human meaning; we do not see the effects of what we do, the outcomes of our actions, or the forces that exceed our choices. Such irony is cosmic irony, or the irony of fate.

—Claire Colebrook, *Irony: The New Critical Idiom* (2004)

Irony is the result of the human capacity for mental detachment from the stream of experience. Because of this capacity, human beings are able to step back from the rush of sensory experience and render it an object of contemplation.

—Glenn S. Holland, *Divine Irony* (2000)

Irony is really only hypocrisy with style.

—Barbara Everett, *Looking for Richard* (1996)

After crying, one puts on dark glasses to hide one's swollen red eyes and save dignity. . . . The glasses suggest the presence of a critical situation whose unsuitable aspect is masked at once. Whoever puts them on wants, on the one hand, to receive sympathy for the uneasiness alluded to and, on the other hand, to arouse admiration for succeeding in not exhibiting such discomfort and for avoiding being too upset by it. In the same way, irony can be likened to a pair of "dark glasses," "uncovering" what it apparently hides. Moreover, just as dark glasses "conceal what they display," irony is a strategy for indirect speech. It is a "meaning-full" mask, and it has the prerogative of rendering flexible the borders of the area of meaning, allowing for their negotiation in accordance with the situation.

—Luigi Anolli et al., "Behind Dark Glasses: Irony As a
    Strategy for Indirect Communication," *Genetic, Social &
    General Psychology Monographs*, February 1, 2002

Paradoxically . . . the people most likely to know the literal definition of irony are the people least likely to appreciate it in its modern form.

—Jonah Goldberg, *National Review*, April 28, 1999

Irony
Versus . . .

There are those who insist on a strict definition of irony, while others are less demanding. It's prescriptivists versus descriptivists in an age-old semiotic dispute. Prescriptivists maintain that linguistic permissiveness is an agent of ignorance, that effective communication requires precision and predictability. For descriptivists, who see language as an evolving entity, the meanings of words are determined by usage, the sole arbiter of legitimacy. It's a battle that neither side can win because the combatants fail to distinguish among the many forms of irony, or even between its two most common varieties: verbal irony, saying one thing and meaning another, and ambient or cosmic irony, that fateful disjunction between expectation and reality at the core of human existence. But even without such ideological disputes, defining irony is a delicate enterprise. We can say what it *isn't* with more confidence, so let us distinguish irony from various "confusables."

IRONY VERSUS COINCIDENCE

Irony involves incongruity between what is expected and what actually happens; coincidence merely denotes spatial or temporal proximity. It is ironic that Beethoven was deaf, but merely coincidental that while two members of ZZ Top, Billy F. Gibbons and Dusty Hill, have long beards, the third member, Frank *Beard,* is clean shaven.

> A lot of people don't realize what's really going on. They view life as a bunch of unconnected incidences and things. They don't realize that there's this like lattice of coincidence that lays on top of everything. I'll give you an example, show you what I mean. Suppose you're thinking about a plate of shrimp. Suddenly somebody will say like "plate" or "shrimp" or "plate of shrimp" out of the blue, no explanation. No point in looking for one either. It's all part of a cosmic unconsciousness.
>
> —From *Repo Man* (1984, screenplay by Alex Cox)

IRONY VERSUS HYPOCRISY

A lot of what passes for irony these days is merely hypocrisy. For example, when it was revealed that William Bennett, author of *The Book of Virtues,* had a secret gambling habit, more than one commentator termed the *irony* "delicious," and it was indeed a pleasure to see such a breathtaking hypocrite get his comeuppance, even though Bennett was publicly unrepentant. But it wasn't irony; it was only hypocrisy. (It *was* ironic when, on *The Daily Show,* Jon Stewart commended Bennett for his indignation and for "standing up to the William Bennetts of the world.")

It was said to be "ironic" but, again, it was just hypocritical, when Linda Chavez, President Bush's nominee for Labor Secretary, was forced to withdraw from consideration after it was alleged that she had employed an illegal alien. Chavez had publicly criticized Zoe Baird, President Clinton's nominee for Attorney General, for failing to make Social Security payments for a nanny she'd employed. Bonus hypocrisy: At the news conference announcing her withdrawal Chavez said, "I do believe that Zoe Baird was treated unfairly."

Irony or *ironic* can be handy code when you can't come right out and call a public figure a hypocrite. Thus did *The New York Times* columnist Maureen Dowd point out the "irony" of Senator John McCain's raising soft money to finance his campaign against soft money.

IRONY VERSUS SARCASM

Irony is subtle, sarcasm blunt:

> Irony must not be confused with sarcasm, which is direct: Sarcasm means precisely what it says, but in a sharp, bitter, cutting, caustic, or acerb manner; it is the

instrument of indignation, a weapon of offence, whereas irony is one of the vehicles of wit. In Locke's "If ideas were innate, it would save much trouble to many worthy persons," *worthy* is ironical; the principal clause as a whole is sarcastic—as also is the complete sentence. Both are instruments of satire and vituperation.

— Eric Partridge, *Usage and Abusage: A Guide to Good English* (1995 revised edition)

People who don't get irony interpret it as sarcasm.

— Douglas Coupland, "The Post Modern Ironic Wink," *To The Best of Our Knowledge*, Wisconsin Public Radio, June 26, 2005

Irony is essentially constructive, sarcasm malicious. Which doesn't mean sarcasm can't be fun:

To the Sports Editor:
Aren't we just imposing our North American concepts of chronology and numbers in insisting that a Dominican youth have the right birthday in order to credit his performance in the Little League World Series? Certainly in the postmodern era, we should understand that people in other parts of the world don't necessarily share our values. Regardless of his birth date, Danny Almonte's feat in pitching a perfect game and striking out 16 of 18 batters will live in history. It belongs right up there with

the feats of that other great New York athlete, Rosie Ruiz.

—William Tucker, *The New York Times*, September 2, 2001

IRONY VERSUS CYNICISM

Irony discriminates; cynicism does not.

The cynic, harboring at least a residual sense of his own superiority, stays home and denounces callow and frivolous party-goers. The ironist goes to the party and, while refusing to be quite *of* it, gets off the best line of the evening.

—Jedediah Purdy, *For Common Things: Irony, Trust, and Commitment in America Today* (1999)

I am the most uncynical person on Earth. I'm ironic. I admit that. I'm Joe Irony. But people confuse irony with cynicism, which is like battery acid. It just wrecks everything.

—Douglas Coupland, quoted by Steve Rabey, *The Cleveland Plain Dealer*, March 11, 2000

IRONY VERSUS EUPHEMISM

Euphemism conceals, irony reveals, albeit by stating the opposite. Political correctness, that virulent strain of euphemism, often generates irony, as when, during the 1992 Rodney King riots ("rebellion" in some reportage), a Los Angeles TV newsperson referred to thugs who attacked white motorists as "community leaders," even though they called *themselves* "gang members."

IRONY VERSUS BULLSHIT

In his 2005 bestseller, *On Bullshit,* Harry G. Frankfurt, Professor of Philosophy Emeritus at Princeton University, deplores the spread of bullshit in American culture. Professor Frankfurt defines a "bullshitter" as someone who doesn't care whether what he says is true or false. Irony, on the other hand, is a means of reaching or expressing the truth. The bullshitter disregards the truth; the ironist respects it. Bonus irony: *On Bullshit,* with its measured academic prose punctuated by the word *bullshit,* is an elegantly ironic book.

Forms of Irony

Irony resists categorization, but a few varieties can be distinguished.

AMBIENT IRONY (AKA SITUATIONAL IRONY, COSMIC IRONY, EXISTENTIAL IRONY, METAPHYSICAL IRONY, TRAGIC IRONY, THE IRONY OF FATE)

Irony exists in nature. It's part of the human condition; it permeates reality like radiation from the Big Bang. Ambient irony happens, whether created by God or Destiny or dumb luck. It results from the difference between what we want and what we get.

> Man proposes, but God disposes.
> —Thomas à Kempis, *Imitation of Christ* (circa 1418)

If a person who indulges in gluttony is a glutton, and a person who commits a felony is a felon, then God is an iron.

—Spider Robinson, *God Is an Iron* (1977)

It is ironic that the one thing that all religions recognize as separating us from our creator—our very self-consciousness—is also the one thing that divides us from our fellow creatures. It was a bitter birthday present from evolution.

—Annie Dillard, *Pilgrim at Tinker Creek* (1974)

It is after you have lost your teeth that you can afford to buy steaks.

—Pierre-Auguste Renoir (attributed)

How is one to live a moral and compassionate existence when one is fully aware of the blood, the horror inherent in life, when one finds darkness not only in one's culture but within oneself? If there is a stage at which an individual life becomes truly adult, it must be when one grasps the irony in its unfolding and accepts responsibility for a life lived in the midst of such paradox. One must live in the middle of contradiction, because if all contradiction were eliminated at once life would collapse. There are simply no answers to some of the great pressing questions. You continue to live them out, making your life a worthy expression of leaning into the light.

—Barry Lopez, *Arctic Dreams* (1986)

If irony isn't literally wired into the human brain, it seems an inevitable response to the human condition. The original ironic juxtaposition, after all, is the spirit plunked down in the material world—a brief sample of the eternal popped into the mechanical drum track of time. Unless somebody figures out how to get comfortable with that, irony's going to be with us until the whole mess comes crashing down. Oh, well. At least we get the last laugh.

—David Gates, "Will We Ever Get Over Irony?" *Newsweek,* January 1, 2000

AMICABLE IRONY

Ritual irony among friends, as when guys insult each other affectionately, or when fellow members of the same race or ethnic group greet each other with ethnic slurs. (No examples will be supplied.)

AUTO-IRONY (AKA SELF-IRONY, SELF-REFLEXIVE IRONY, SELF-PARODY)

Feigned self-effacement; irony that seeks to disarm one's critics by making fun of oneself. The auto-ironist says, in effect, "Hey, I don't take myself seriously—I'm a regular person, just like you!" The 1950s movie actor George Hamilton, for example, has kept himself marginally in the public eye for decades by kidding his own narcissism. William Shatner is another master of auto-irony, as seen on TV in Priceline commercials, and as evidenced by his CD, *Has Been,* recorded at a time when the former *Star Trek* star was widely regarded a has-been. In 2006, Shatner sold his kidney stone for twenty-five thousand dollars, which he donated to Habitat for Humanity, then had the following exchange on CNN's *Showbiz Tonight:*

A.J. Hammer: Twenty-five thousand dollars is nothing to sneeze at. . . .

Shatner: If you sneezed at it, we might be able to sell that, too.

In the *auto-ironic cameo,* a celebrity appears in a movie as himself and mocks his public image, as if to say, "Let me make fun of myself before someone else does." Neil Diamond revitalized his career that way. Though he'd sold over 100 million records and was still a top-drawing concert performer, Diamond had long been a figure of fun, what with the shiny shirts, triumphant hair, and lyrics that seem translated from a foreign language. Hard-core rockers never took him seriously, and *Rolling Stone* dubbed him "the Jewish Elvis." After all, he'd recorded the soundtrack to *Jonathan Livingston Seagull,* done that schmaltzy "You Don't Bring Me Flowers" duet with Barbra Streisand, and cowritten and performed "Heartlight," inspired by the 1982 movie *E.T. the Extra-Terrestrial.* Baby Boomers' *parents* liked Neil Diamond's music, but Boomers themselves listened to it ironically, or not at all. Then he did an auto-ironic cameo in the 2001 film *Saving Silverman,* in which the main characters play in a Neil Diamond cover band. The appearance endeared him to a generation of under-forty fans for whom Neil Diamond was suddenly . . . cool. Bonus irony: For once it's the Gen Xers who are clueless.

Auto-ironic television commercials flatter the intelligence of the audience, pretending to let viewers in on the joke so they can congratulate themselves on their superiority, not only to people who fall for commercials, but also to those who create them. A subgenre uses 1960s and '70s hits as background music in an attempt to have it both ways, that is, simultaneously appeal nostalgically to oldsters and ironically to youngsters.

DEAD IRONY

Familiarity displaces irony so that some ironies erode over time and finally disappear. Thus did *underwhelm* begin as an ironic nonce word, gradually gain acceptance through usage, and eventually emerge irony-free. The process isn't exclusively verbal:

> At some point, after you continually act a certain way to "ironically comment" on something, well, that just becomes you. Even if you have learned to isolate it out of the context it is commonly used in, it's your mannerism now. Case(s) in point: (1) **Joke dancing.** If you keep joke dancing, you are in fact practicing and one day, you'll forget how you used to dance and most importantly, your friends will forget how you used to dance. You will dance exactly in the way you have been mocking, because really you've been practicing on the dance floor. (2) **Woo-wooing.** If you say "woo-woo" as an expression of excitement to poke fun at frat and sorority types that do that at shows, parades, etc. (basically anywhere there is a crowd), you may find yourself being (disappointingly) the person in your group who is the "woo-woo" person. The only save being that you, of course, don't do this behavior in the expected context (crowds), but instead do it only in unexpected contexts, such as a small group of three at a nice restaurant. So it is still funny, but only just. Don't do it on a dance floor though, or you've become the joke dancing "woo-woo" person.
>
> —Magpie, posted June 22, 2005, thisistenspeed.blogspot.com

DOUBLE ENTENDRE

A classic form of irony in which there are two meanings, one of which is risqué.

The Barrison Sisters
(www.laughingravy21.com)

One of the earliest examples of double entendre in American culture was the late nineteenth-century vaudeville act, the Barrison Sisters. They danced, raising their skirts slightly, and asking the audience: "Would you like to see my pussy?" After an enthusiastic response,

they would raise up their skirts, revealing live kittens
secured over their crotches.

—Wikipedia, on July 20, 2006, at
wikipedia.org/wiki/Double_entendre

DRAMATIC IRONY

The audience understands the situation while the characters
are ignorant or believe the opposite, so that plot developments
have a double meaning, one for the character and another for
the audience. The classic case is Sophocles' *Oedipus the King,*
in which the audience, but not Oedipus, knows that the man
Oedipus killed was his father and the woman he married is his
mother, so it's ironic when Oedipus lays a curse on the killer,
unaware that he's actually cursing himself. The irony increases
our tension and involvement: Because we know Oedipus' im-
pending fate, we would not act as he does. Indeed, if only we
could *warn* him . . . before it's too late! Dramatic irony remains an important storytelling element: In horror movies, for
example, when an unsuspecting teenager is about to enter a
room where a homicidal maniac lurks, audiences want to
shout (and, alas, increasingly do shout), "DON'T GO IN
THERE!"

FORCED IRONY (AKA FAILED IRONY, FAUX IRONY, FALSE IRONY, PSEUDO IRONY)

The cynical use of irony for financial gain, as evidenced by clothed Weimaraners or the corny T-shirts sold in the Wireless Catalog:

"Some days, it's not even worth chewing through the restraints."

"DIJON VU: The feeling that you've already had this mustard before."

"Manure occureth."

"I don't skinny dip, I chunky dunk."

"I don't want to. I don't have to. You can't make me. I'm retired."

Note: A master ironist would wear a Wireless Catalog T-shirt *meta-ironically*. Most people he encounters would not appreciate the meta-irony and might well presume him witless, but the master ironist would revel in the misunderstanding, because being misunderstood by the unironic is the raison d'être of the master ironist.

IRONIC CONSUMPTION

Acquisition of pop-culture artifacts from bygone eras not for their intrinsic worth but for their very lameness, for example such kitsch memorabilia as Lava lamps, sushi shower curtains, Rat Pack postcards, Robert Goulet CDs, velvet Elvises, and so forth.

IRONIC TWIST

The wry reversal at the end of a story that delivers the moral. Atop the list of stories with famous ironic twists we find O. Henry's "Gift of the Magi" (1906), in which Della and Jim, a poor but happy young couple, scrape together money to buy each other expensive Christmas gifts. Della decides to buy Jim a platinum fob chain for his prized pocket watch. To pay for it, she sells her beautiful long tresses to a hair goods store, hoping Jim will still love her with short hair. Jim comes home on Christmas and is stunned by Della's appearance. She rushes to him, assuring him that her hair will grow back quickly. Jim takes a small package from his coat and assures Della that nothing could change his feelings for her. When Della opens the package, she's astonished to find the set of jeweled, tortoiseshell combs she'd been admiring in a store window. Regaining her composure, Della hands Jim her gift, and when he opens it, she asks for his watch to see how it will look with the new fob. But Jim sinks to the couch. "Let's put our Christmas presents away and keep 'em a while," he says. "They're too nice to use just at present. I sold the watch to get the money to buy your combs."

In Guy de Maupassant's short story "The Necklace" ("*La Parure,*" 1885), Monsieur Loisel, a minor bureaucrat, and his pretty wife, Mathilde, are invited to an official reception. When Mathilde complains of having nothing suitable to wear, he gives her the money he's been saving for a hunting trip to buy a new gown. As the great occasion approaches, Mathilde worries that she has no jewelry to complement the gown and her husband, out of cash, suggests she borrow jewelry from her friend Madame Forestier, who indeed lends her a fine diamond necklace. Mathilde is the belle of the ball, but the necklace mysteriously disappears. Rather than face Madame Forestier with the truth, Monsieur Loisel goes deep into debt to buy a replacement. To repay his creditors, he takes part-time jobs and the couple moves to a smaller apartment. Over time the pretty young Mathilde, now forced to do housework and dicker with shopkeepers over every centime, turns into an old hag. After years of penury, the couple finally pay off the debt. Then one day Mathilde encounters Madame Forestier and tells her of the loss of the necklace and the hardships the couple endured to replace it. Madame Forestier takes her by the hand and says, "My poor Mathilde, you suffered for nothing: My necklace wasn't real, just a paste imitation."

In W. Somerset Maugham's short story "The Verger" (1929), the newly appointed vicar of St. Peter's in London's Neville Square decides that the church's longtime verger must either learn to read and write or lose his job. The verger resigns, declaring he's too old to learn. On his way home he runs out of cigarettes, but can't find a tobacconist on a long street with all sorts of other shops. Seizing the opportunity, he rents a small space and sells tobacco, newspapers, and sweets. The shop thrives, he opens a second, then a third, and soon owns a whole chain. One day, making a large deposit, he admits to the bank manager that he can't read or write.

"Do you mean to say that you've built up this important business and amassed a fortune . . . without being able to read or write? Good God, man, what would you be now if you had been able to?"

"I can tell you that sir," he replies with a little smile. "I'd be verger of St. Peter's, Neville Square."

In the 1958 *Alfred Hitchcock Presents* episode "Lamb to the Slaughter" (teleplay and story by Roald Dahl), a suburban housewife (Barbara Bel Geddes) bludgeons her philandering husband to death with a frozen leg of lamb, calmly calls the police, then serves the investigating officers the murder weapon for dinner. In the final scene, as Lieutenant Noonan (Harold J. Stone) cuts into the meat, he muses on the phantom weapon: "For all we know," he says, "it could be right under our very noses."

In the 1959 *Twilight Zone* episode "Time Enough at Last" (teleplay by Rod Serling from a story by Lyn Venable), Burgess Meredith plays bookish bank teller Henry Bemis, a little man with thick glasses whose insatiable appetite for the printed word is frustrated by a shrewish wife and a tyrannical boss. Henry takes refuge during lunch breaks in the bank's vault for an hour of uninterrupted reading. One day he is knocked unconscious by a giant concussion. He awakens to find that he's the last man on earth, having been protected by the vault from a nuclear holocaust. Wandering through the desolated city, he finds abundant food and shelter, but the loneliness overwhelms him, and just as he's about to put a gun to his head he notices the ruins of a . . . library!

Burgess Meredith as Henry Bemis
(CBS/Photofest)

Cut to: stacks of books piled high on the library's front steps and Henry giddy with delight over years of future reading. But as he settles down on the curb with the first book, his glasses slip off and shatter on the pavement, trapping him forever in a blurry world.

A famous poem by Edwin Arlington Robinson set in a fictional New England town distills a life into sixteen lines with a wrenching ironic twist at the end:

Richard Cory

Whenever Richard Cory went down town,
We people on the pavement looked at him:
He was a gentleman from sole to crown,
Clean favored, and imperially slim.

And he was always quietly arrayed,
And he was always human when he talked;
But still he fluttered pulses when he said,
"Good-morning," and he glittered when he
    walked.

And he was rich—yes, richer than a king,
And admirably schooled in every grace:
In fine, we thought he was everything
To make us wish that we were in his place.

So on we worked, and waited for the light,
And went without the meat, and cursed the
    bread;
And Richard Cory, one calm summer night,
Went home and put a bullet through his head.

  —Edwin Arlington Robinson, *The Children of the Night*
  (1897)

On a lighter note, the drama critic turned Hollywood script-writer Samuel Hoffenstein (1890–1947) penned the following pleasant surprise:

Your little hands,
Your little feet,
Your little mouth—
Oh, God, how sweet!
Your little nose,
Your little ears,
Your eyes, that shed
Such little tears!
Your little voice,
So soft and kind;
Your little soul,
Your little mind!

—Samuel Hoffenstein, "Love-Songs, at Once Tender
and Informative—An Unusual Combination in Verses of
This Character," *The Complete Poetry of Samuel
Hoffenstein* (1954)

IRONY DEFICIENCY

Irony.

—Los Angeles–based British actor Tim Curry, when asked
what he missed most about the U.K.

It is often claimed that Americans have no sense of irony.
The British certainly think so. As do some Americans:

I don't think America is at heart, so to speak, an ironic country. We might benefit from more of the Socratic kind of irony. Our current variety, though, is not much better than meretricious sarcasm.
　　—Jedediah Purdy, *Slate*, September 22, 1999

We are are a straightforward and self-righteous people, so we are rather good at viciousness, but lacking in irony.
　　—David Mamet, *The Guardian*, November 28, 2003

The notion that Americans are irony-impaired is a canard. We've shown a flair for irony ever since our beginnings as a nation: "Yankee Doodle" was first sung by the British to mock the disheveled colonials, but American revolutionaries adopted it as an *ironic* anthem.

And according to H. L. Mencken, a critic of the American character and certainly no jingoist:

For the student interested in the biology of language, as opposed to its paleontology, there is endless material in the racy neologisms of American, and particularly in its new compounds and novel verbs. Nothing could exceed the brilliancy of such inventions as *joy-ride, high-brow, road-louse, sob-sister, frame-up, loan-shark, nature-faker, stand-patter, lounge-lizard, hash-foundry, buzz-wagon, has-been, end-seat-hog, shoot-the-chutes,* and *grape-juice diplomacy.* They are bold; they are vivid; they have humor; they meet genuine needs. *Joy-ride* is already going over into English, and no wonder. There is absolutely no synonym for it; to convey its idea in orthodox English would take a whole sentence. And so, too, with certain single words of metaphorical origin: *barrel* for large and illicit wealth, *pork* for unnecessary and dishonest appropriations of public money, *joint* for illegal liquor-house, *tenderloin* for a gay and dubious neighborhood. Many of these, and of the new compounds with them, belong to the vocabulary of disparagement, *e.g., bone-head, skunk, bug, jay, lobster, boob, mutt, gas (empty talk), geezer, piker, baggage-smasher, hash-slinger, clock-watcher, four-flusher, coffin-nail, chin-music, batty,* and *one-horse.* Here an essential character of the American shows itself: his tendency to combat the disagreeable with irony, to heap ridicule upon what he is suspicious of or doesn't understand.

—H. L. Mencken, *The American Language* (1920)

What was true almost a century ago is true today: Contemporary Americans still appreciate irony, but in its proper place, not in a constant barrage (like you get from Brits). Americans are *doers.* Get too ironic on the job, you run the risk of being thought rude and, worse, not a "team player." That said, if Americans didn't get irony, *The Simpsons* wouldn't still be on the air. Anyway, it depends on the venue. The two coasts tend to be ironic while the heartland does not. Harvard is ironic, Oklahoma State is not. Key West is ironic, West Point is not:

> Cadets entering West Point step into an irony-free zone,
> a place where sarcasm has been fought to a standstill.
> And an irony-free zone turns out to be an immense relief
> for human beings: a relief not to have to worry about
> sounding foolish or whether somebody's statement has
> a subtext; a relief to accept the apparent meaning and
> move on.
>
> —David Lipsky, *Absolutely American: Four Years at West
> Point* (2003)

Utah will never, ever be ironic.

Irony deficiency is directly proportional to the strength of the political commitment or religious fervor. True believers of all persuasions are irony-deficient:

> The only people who take the Bible literally are
> fundamentalists and atheists.
>
> —Andy Kindler, standup routine

Brutal dictators are irony-deficient—take Hitler, Stalin, Kim Jong-il, and Saddam Hussein, a world-class vulgarian whose art collection consisted of kitsch paintings displayed unironically.

Totalitarian regimes and theocracies are irony-deficient, of course, but so are democracies, where, though politicians are ironic in the sense that they're congenital dissemblers, it is unwise for them to consciously commit irony, even in the U.K.:

A typical painting from Saddam Hussein's
art collection
(AP Photo/John Moore)

The first thing a fledgling MP should be told on arrival at
Westminster is never indulge in irony.

It may sound fine in the Commons, accompanied by
nods and winks, but when you read it in Hansard in the
cold light of the following day, it simply looks barmy
and, like statements made to the police, may be used
against you as evidence.

A cautionary tale: Chris Patten, the former Bath MP,

when he was Environment Secretary, listened patiently to a Labour Member describing his party's alternative to the Council Tax.

At the end of this, Mr. Patten exclaimed, his voice loaded with sarcasm: "I'm gobsmacked!" [utterly astonished, astounded] which was meant to mean "I am not at all gobsmacked."

Too late! The words "I'm gobsmacked!" were splashed all over the following day's papers. And there is nothing more pathetic than a politician whimpering afterwards: "But I was being ironic."

The message clearly has not got through to the Deputy Prime Minister, John Prescott. When asked whether he was considering retiring, he said: "I keep going. It's still better than working for a living." Careful, John! The Tories could nail you for this. But then, on second thoughts, perhaps the man was not trying to be ironic, after all. . . .

—*Europe Intelligence Wire*, July 21, 2004

META-IRONY

Irony that refers to the ironies associated with irony. For example, to offer as an instance of irony the fact that Lou Gehrig died of Lou Gehrig's disease is either to practice meta-irony, or to be incredibly obtuse.

It's impossible to write or read about irony without either becoming ironic, falling victim to irony, or both. Schlegel calls this effect "Unverstandlichkeit," the impossibility of understanding. Kierkegaard provides us with a metaphor: Irony, like the greedy witch from a Danish fairy tale, must eventually devour even its own stomach.

—Jennifer Thompson, "Irony: a Few Simple Definitions,"
    Teachers' Resource Web

Irony can be pretty damned ironic.

—William Shatner as Commander Buck Murdock,
    Airplane II: The Sequel (1982, screenplay by Ken
    Finkleman)

While the author is self-conscious about being self-referential, he is also knowing about that self-conscious self-referentiality. Further, and if you're one of those people who can tell what's going to happen before it actually happens, you've predicted the next element here: He also plans to be clearly, obviously aware of his knowingness about his self-consciousness of self-referentiality. Further, he is fully cognizant, way ahead of you, in terms of knowing about and fully admitting the gimmickry inherent in all this, and will preempt your claim of the book's irrelevance due to said gimmickry by saying that the gimmickry is simply a device, a defense, to obscure the black, blinding, murderous rage and sorrow at the core of this whole story, which is both too black and blinding to look at.

—Dave Eggers, *A Heartbreaking Work of Staggering Genius* (2000)

"How ironic is *that*?" isn't really a question, it's a meta-ironic statement; it doesn't seek an answer, it provides one, that is, "It's *very* ironic."

Wah, wah, wah, waahhhh, the muted trumpet notes that punctuated rare ironic moments on 1950s television, were to sitcom irony what canned laughter is to sitcom comedy. The twenty-first-century meta-ironist might voice it to call attention to an ironic moment in everyday life:

Civilian: I bought a suit with two pairs of pants and burned a hole in the jacket!
Meta-ironist: *Wah, wah, wah, waahhhh . . .*

MORISSETTIAN IRONY

Irony based on a misapprehension of irony, that is, no irony at all. Named for pop singer Alanis Morissette, whose hit single "Ironic" mislabels coincidence and inconvenience as irony.

ORWELLIAN IRONY

Self-contradictory or grossly false propaganda used by a government to deceive and manipulate the public. The name derives from George Orwell, in whose dystopian novel *Nineteen Eighty-Four* (1949) the world is dominated by three perpetually warring superpowers, one of which is Oceania, a totalitarian state ruled by Big Brother where "thoughtcrimes" are punishable by death and "Newspeak" and "Doublethink" replace logic and truth. Three slogans promulgated by the "Ministry of Truth" are repeated constantly and displayed everywhere:

WAR IS PEACE

FREEDOM IS SLAVERY

IGNORANCE IS STRENGTH

The phrase "It was necessary to destroy the village in order to save it," originally attributed to an American general in Vietnam, is often invoked as classic Orwellian irony. Other examples: The Japanese Family Leave Act of 1942, mandating the arrest and imprisonment of Japanese-American citizens; the B-36 Peacemaker nuclear bomber; and the Atoms for Peace program, which enabled the worldwide spread of fissionable material, eventually to such regimes as the Democratic People's Republic of Korea, one of the most repressive dictatorships in history.

As far as I can tell, the Clear Skies Initiative is basically to clear the skies of birds.

—Al Franken in a speech at Jimmy Carter Library, November 30, 2005

POSTMODERN IRONY

Postmodern irony is allusive, multilayered, preemptive, cynical, and above all, nihilistic. It assumes that everything is subjective and nothing means what it says. It's a sneering, world-weary, *bad* irony, a mentality that condemns before it can be condemned, preferring cleverness to sincerity and quotation to originality. Postmodern irony rejects tradition, but offers nothing in its place.

Postmodern irony first appeared in postmodern fiction, which began, according to the postmodern novelist David Foster Wallace, with a "rehabilitative agenda," that is, as an ironic weapon against hypocrisy. But the irony quickly devolved into a hip mode of social discourse among the young and the marginalized—a way of looking cool, a mechanism for avoiding important issues and a substitute for civic, religious, and moral values.

The ironic individual practices a style of speech and behavior that avoids all appearance of naïveté—of naïve devotion, belief, or hope. He subtly protests the inadequacy of the things he says, the gestures he makes, the acts he performs. By the inflection of his voice, the expression of his face, and the motion of his body, he signals that he is aware of all the ways he may be thought silly or jejune, and that he might even think so himself. His wariness becomes a mistrust of language itself. He disowns his own words.

—Jedediah Purdy, *For Common Things: Irony, Trust, and Commitment in America Today* (1999)

Postmodern agenda: The peep show is the art form; the voyeur is the protagonist; the goal is excitement from a safe distance; the alibi is that it's all ironic.

—Mason Cooley, *City Aphorisms, Fourteenth Selection* (1994)

Pity poor irony. Irony used to be a rebellious stance, a way of looking at an orderly world through a cracked mirror, a way of busting balloons filled with pompous hot air. But what does one do when irony becomes the norm? When there is no orderly world to mock? When everyone wants to be Groucho and no one is willing to play Margaret Dumont? You end up with a world in which everyone wants to be the hippest one in the room, in which comedy becomes so superior and distant it seldom stoops to being funny. A world in which irreverence itself becomes meaningless, because nothing is revered. A world like the one we're in now.

—Phoef Sutton, *San Francisco Chronicle*, May 21, 2000

ROMANTIC IRONY

A theory posited by the German philosopher Friedrich von Schlegel (1772–1829) based on the assumption that irony inheres in the very fact of being an artist, and that ambivalence is the only viable stance in a paradoxical world. (The name derives from *roman,* the French word for "novel.") Sometimes called *philosophical irony,* it seeks to triangulate the truth by assuming a variety of mutually exclusive points of view. The novelist employing romantic irony stays detached, noncommittal, nonjudgmental, sometimes even revealing himself as the creator of a literary illusion.

The romantic-irony theory greatly influenced the English Romantic poets, especially Samuel Taylor Coleridge, whose "Rime of the Ancient Mariner" is written from two perspectives: the poem's narrative itself, plus a running commentary. Henry Fielding often interrupts the storyline to comment on the action in *Joseph Andrews,* as does Jonathan Swift in *A Tale of a Tub,* as does Bugs Bunny when he faces the audience and asks, "Ironic, ain't it?" Philip Roth's seriocomic, metafictional, multinarrational, double-self-contradictory fiction may be the ultimate manifestation of romantic irony.

> The dream, surely, that we all have, is to write this beautiful paragraph that actually is describing something but at the same time in another voice is writing a commentary on its own creation, without

having to be a story about a writer.

—Ian McEwan, *The Believer Book of Writers Talking to Writers*, edited by Vendela Vida (2005)

Romantic Irony [is] the irony of the fully conscious artist whose art is the ironical presentation of the ironic position of the fully conscious artist. The artist is in an ironic position for several reasons: In order to write well he must be both creative and critical, subjective and objective, enthusiastic and realistic, emotional and rational, unconsciously inspired and a conscious artist; his work purports to be about the world and yet is fiction; he feels an obligation to give a true or complete account of reality but he knows this is impossible, reality being incomprehensibly vast, full of contradictions, and in a continual state of becoming, so that even a true account would be immediately falsified as soon as it was completed. The only possibility for a real artist is to stand apart from his work and at the same time incorporate this awareness of his ironic position into the work itself and so create something which will, if a novel, not simply be a story but rather the telling of a story complete with the author and the narrating, the reader and the reading, the style and the choosing of the style, the fiction and its distance from fact, so that we shall regard it as being both art and life.

—D. C. Muecke, *Irony* (1970)

SOCRATIC IRONY

Sometimes called "dialectical irony," Socratic irony is a strategy for refuting dogma. In the Platonic dialogues, Socrates assumes the role of *eiron*, a sly dissembler who feigns naïveté by asking seemingly foolish questions that slowly but surely trap his interlocutors by their own admissions.

Socratic irony was a profession of ignorance. What Socrates represented as an ignorance and a weakness in himself was in fact a non-committal attitude toward any dogma, however accepted or imposing, that had not been carried back to and shown to be based on first principles. The two parties in his audience were, first, the dogmatists moved by pity or contempt to enlighten this ignorance, and secondly, those who knew their Socrates and set themselves to watch the familiar game in which learning should be turned inside out by simplicity.

—H. W. Fowler, *A Dictionary of Modern English Usage,*
second edition, revised by Sir Ernest Gowers (1965)

Some go so far as to say that Socrates' ironic personality inaugurated a peculiarly Western sensibility. His irony, or his capacity *not* to accept everyday values and concepts but live in a state of perpetual question, is the birth of philosophy, ethics, and consciousness.

—Claire Colebrook, *Irony: The New Critical Idiom* (2004)

UNDERSTATEMENT

Understatement can border on irony, as when Mark Twain writes to a correspondent, "the report of my death was an exaggeration"; or when, in *The Wizard of Oz,* Dorothy says, upon suddenly finding herself amid Technicolored splendor, "Toto, I have a feeling we're not in Kansas anymore"; or when Swift writes in *A Tale of a Tub* (1699): "Last week I saw a woman flayed, and you will hardly believe how much it altered her person for the worse." Extreme case of ironic understatement: Emperor Hirohito ruled Japan as a living god until August 14, 1945, when, with his cities destroyed by American bombs, his armies vanquished, and his nation's industrial capacity obliterated, he addressed his subjects on the radio to announce Japan's surrender:

> Indeed, we declared war on America and Britain out of our sincere desire to insure Japan's self-preservation and the stabilization of East Asia, it being far from our thought either to infringe upon the sovereignty of other nations or to embark upon territorial aggrandizement.
>
> But now the war has lasted for nearly four years. Despite the best that has been done by everyone—the gallant fighting of our military and naval forces, the diligence and assiduity of our servants of the State, and the devoted service of our 100,000,000 people—*the war situation has developed not necessarily to Japan's*

*advantage, while the general trends of the world have
all turned against her interest.* [emphasis added]

Japan's Empress Nagako displayed a similar flair for understatement when she wrote in a letter a few weeks later, "Unfortunately, the B-29 is a splendid plane."

VERBAL IRONY (AKA RHETORICAL IRONY)

The most common form of irony, it's the practice of saying one thing but meaning the opposite with the intent of being understood as meaning the opposite, as in, "Nice weather we're having" on a rainy day or, "With all due respect," when none is due.

> People frequently use a simple form of verbal irony to forge bonds with a new acquaintance. The listener is pleased to get the joke, however simple, and the speaker is pleased to have made it, and to have pleased the listener.
> —Jennifer Thompson, "Irony: A Few Simple Definitions,"
> *Teachers' Resource Web*

VILRONY

According to the *Urban Dictionary* (urbandictionary.com), this form of irony has two distinct meanings: "1. The act of tricking someone into having sex with you just so that you can do something harmful to them. *He committed vilrony when he hand-cuffed his girlfriend in a sexual way, but then proceeded to steal her money and leave her handcuffed to the chair.* 2. Vinyl records purchased out of irony. *Ever seen the* Play It Again *LP by the Alan Gardiner Accordion Band? Boy, that's a great piece of vilrony.*"

VISUAL IRONY

(Photo by Jon Winokur)

In visual irony, an image or object contradicts itself, either intentionally (for example, flames painted on a minivan) or acci-

(Getty Images/Margaret Bourke-White)

dentally, as in a 1937 Margaret Bourke-White photograph ostensibly showing a Depression Era breadline ironically juxtaposed with a billboard touting American prosperity. Bonus irony: In fact, the people are not welfare recipients, but victims of a flood.

Sometimes an image combines with circumstances to produce visual irony, as in the case of the famous photo of a smiling Harry S. Truman holding up the *Chicago Daily Tribune* with the headline, DEWEY DEFEATS TRUMAN. It is one of the most iconic—and ironic—images in American political history.

The headline is wrong, of course. Truman won the 1948 presidential election over New York's Governor Thomas E. Dewey by 4 percent of the vote, despite public opinion surveys predicting a landslide for Dewey. Truman, who became

Harry Truman after winning the presidency,
holding the newspaper that predicted his defeat
(AP Photo/Byron Rollins)

President when Franklin D. Roosevelt died in office in April
of 1945, had been under constant attack from the press, Republicans, and even fellow Democrats for his performance in
office. His support of civil rights legislation and tough stance
against Communism had splintered the Democratic Party,
and as a result, his 1948 presidential campaign was under-
funded. With Strom Thurmond's pro-segregation Dixiecrat
ticket and Henry Wallace's Progressive Party threatening to
siphon off Democratic votes, *The New York Times* declared
Dewey's election a "foregone conclusion," and a *Life* magazine cover ran Dewey's picture over the caption, "The Next
President of the United States." Truman's victory was thus a
huge embarrassment for the press (especially for the *Chicago*

Daily Tribune) and a fiasco for the emerging public polling industry. Asked to comment, a jubilant Truman said, "This is for the books."

Bonus irony 1: The late swing in voter sentiment that tipped the election to Truman probably resulted from poll results favoring Dewey, which made Republicans overconfident but energized Democrats, who intensified last-minute efforts to get their voters to the polls.

Bonus irony 2: In 1999, computer company Dell used a doctored version of the Truman photo in an ad that ran in newspapers across the country. Truman is still seen holding the paper, but the headline is altered to read: DELL LOWERS PRICES. Thus in the context of the image, the headline implies the opposite, that is, that Dell has *raised* prices—clearly the contrary of what the ad was meant to convey.

At the 2000 Republican Convention in Philadelphia, after losing the presidential nomination to what he called a Bush-financed "Death Star," Senator John McCain was brought onstage to the strains of the "Theme from Star Wars" and proceeded to endorse his former nemesis "with a smile so tight you could almost hear the enamel cracking," according to the satirist Will Durst.

The sixteenth-century painting by Leonardo da Vinci (1452–1519) that hangs in the Louvre in Paris is believed to be a portrait of the wife of a merchant named Giacondo, but her famously ambiguous smile may represent Leonardo's ironic view of the human condition.

Mona Lisa
(Corbis)

The Mona Lisa has been interpreted as both a portrait of someone smiling ironically and as an ironical portrait of someone smiling with foolish self-satisfaction.

—D. C. Muecke, *Irony* (1970)

Plastic surgery creates a form of visual irony. Having the nose surgically altered, for example, is literally "dissembling," that is, "disguising or concealing behind a false appearance." As with other forms of cosmetic surgery, the patient either wants to appear younger, or wants to look like someone of a different ethnicity.

Rhinoplasty, one of the most popular forms of cosmetic surgery, was pioneered in the nineteenth century by a Jewish doctor to help women "suffering" from a "Jewish nose." When Fanny Brice had a nose job in 1923, explaining that she had wanted to change her nose from "prominent" to "merely decorative," Dorothy Parker cracked that the comedienne had "cut off her nose to spite her race." But Miss Brice never denied her heritage—she'd made a career performing Jewish material, after all. No, she just wanted her nose to "return to normalcy," she said. Her attitude prefigured that of future generations of Jewish women who, according to a postwar study, underwent rhinoplasty not because they wished to deny their Jewishness, but in order to be accepted as individuals and not stereotyped

Michael Jackson after
multiple rhinoplasties
(Corbis)

Jennifer Grey, before and after rhinoplasty
(Left: Paramount Pictures/Photofest)
(Right: ABC/Photofest)

as members of a particular group. Bonus irony 1: Other ethnics responding to the same survey gave a different reason: Armenian, Greek, and Italian women admitted having nose jobs to avoid being mistaken for Jews. Bonus irony 2: The little turned-up nose so prized by ethnics is the same model that an earlier generation of Irish immigrants had had lengthened in order to fit in.

Scores of public figures have had nose jobs, from former Klan Grand Wizard David Duke to Michael Jackson, whose nose has been hammered so many times it is now removable, to the actress Jennifer Grey who, after notable appearances in *Ferris Bueller's Day Off* (1986) and *Dirty Dancing* (1987) underwent rhinoplasty to advance her career. The surgery achieved the desired cosmetic effect—Grey's new nose was smaller and more in proportion with the rest of her face, but it had the opposite effect on her professional fortunes: The new nose changed her appearance so radically that casting directors no longer recognized her. She had lost her individuality—that special something that made her interesting—and her career stalled.

Bonus irony: Grey later appeared in the short-lived comedy series, *It's Like, You Know . . .* as a struggling actress named Jennifer Grey whose career was curtailed by an ill-advised nose job.

The Annals of Irony

423 B.C.

Greek satirist Aristophanes defines irony as simple lying and relates it to a "slimy, crawling temper."

399 B.C.

In a stark demonstration of the practical limits of Socratic irony, its eponymous inventor is forced to commit suicide.

360 B.C.

First known use of "irony" (in Plato's *Republic*) to describe the sly dissimulation of the Greek philosopher Socrates, an *eiron* who feigns ignorance in order to confound his enemies.

350 B.C.

Greek philosopher Aristotle refers to irony (*eirōnia*) in his *Nichomachean Ethics*.

A.D. 90

In his *Institutio Oratoria,* Roman rhetorician Quintillian defines irony as "saying what is contrary to what is meant."

753 B.C.–A.D. 476

Roman orators make increasing use of irony in public speeches.

1502

First known English use of "irony," by the Order of Crysten Men: "Yronye—of grammare, by the whiche a man sayth one & gyveth to understande the contrarye."

1589

George Puttenham's *Arte of English Poesie* shows appreciation for subtle rhetorical irony by translating "ironia" as "Drie Mock."

I tried to find out what irony really is, and discovered that some ancient writer on poetry had spoken of Ironia, which we call the drye mock, and I cannot think of a better term for it: the drye mock. Not sarcasm, which is like vinegar, or cynicism, which is often the voice of disappointed idealism, but a delicate casting of a cool and illuminating light on life, and thus an enlargement. The ironist is not bitter, he does not seek to undercut everything that seems worthy or serious, he scorns the cheap scoring-off of the wisecracker. He stands, so to speak, somewhat at one side, observes and speaks with a moderation which is occasionally embellished with a flash of controlled exaggeration. He speaks from a certain depth, and thus he is not of the same nature as the wit, who so often speaks from the tongue and no deeper. The wit's desire is to be funny, the ironist is only funny as a secondary achievement.

—Robertson Davies, *The Cunning Man* (1994)

1630

First known English use of the adjective *ironic*, in Ben Jonson's play *The New Inn:* "Most Socratick lady! Or if you will, ironick!"

1755

Samuel Johnson's *Dictionary of the English Language* defines *irony* as "a mode of speech in which the meaning is clearly contrary to the words," giving the example: "Bolingbroke is a holy man." From which readers infer that Johnson deemed Bolingbroke a shit.

1831

Thomas Carlyle foreshadows an irony backlash in his *Sartor Resartus:* "An ironic man . . . more especially an ironic young man . . . may be viewed as a pest to society."

1841

Danish philosopher Søren Kierkegaard publishes *The Concept of Irony,* the first serious examination of the subject.

1878

In his book of aphorisms *Human, All Too Human,* Friedrich Wilhelm Nietzsche notes the alienation of the German people, as evidenced by their increasing use of irony.

1916

The carnage of World War I shatters romantic illusions about chivalry and valor, launching a new age of irony. *The Wipers Times* is the best and most popular of the dozens of satirical trench journals ("trench rags" to the soldiers) produced by individual units and circulated along the Western Front. Its name is both a slang mispronunciation of Ypres, and an allusion to the publication's auxiliary use. Full of poems, short stories, song lyrics, jokes, mock advertisements (one recurring ad is for the "Hotel des Ramparts") and such features as "Things We Want to Know" (for example, "Are we being as offensive as we might be?"), *The Wipers Times* is a rich source of self-protective irony, an outlet for the soldiers' frustration, disillusionment, and horror at the lethal absurdity of trench warfare.

Bonus irony: Though *The Wipers Times* was ironic about the war itself, it unwaveringly affirmed home leave as a welcome relief, even though soldiers found the brief respites stressful and demoralizing.

1921

French ironist Anatole France (Jacques-Anatole-François Thibault, 1844–1924), who once proclaimed irony "the gaiety of reflection and the joy of wisdom," wins the Nobel Prize for literature.

The law, in its majestic equality, forbids the rich as well as the poor to sleep under bridges, to beg in the streets, and to steal bread.

—Anatole France, *The Red Lily* (1894)

1924

Cambridge don I. A. Richards (1893–1979) sparks interest in irony among literary critics on both sides of the Atlantic with his book *Principles of Literary Criticism*.

1926

Ernest Hemingway's novel *The Sun Also Rises* includes a sarcastic rejoinder to a laudatory review of *The Great Gatsby*, in which F. Scott Fitzgerald quotes Anatole France's exhortation to writers, "Let us give to men irony and pity as witnesses and judges":

"Work for the good of all." Bill stepped into his underclothes. "Show irony and pity."

I started out of the room with the tackle-bag, the nets, and the rod case.

"Hey! Come back!"

I put my head in the door.

"Aren't you going to show a little irony and pity?"

I thumbed my nose.

"That's not irony."

As I went downstairs, I heard Bill singing, "Irony and Pity. When you're feeling . . . Oh, give them Irony and give them Pity. Oh, give them Irony. When they're feeling . . . Just a little irony. Just a little pity . . ." He kept on singing until he came downstairs. The tune was: "The Bells Are Ringing for Me and My Gal." I was reading a week-old Spanish paper.

"What's with all this irony and pity?"

"What, don't you know about Irony and Pity?"

"No, who got it up?"

"Everybody. They're mad about it in New York. It's just like the Fratellinis used to be."

The girl came in with the coffee and buttered toast. Or rather, it was bread toasted and buttered.

"Ask her if she's got any jam," Bill said. "Be ironical with her."

"Have you got any jam?"

"That's not ironical. I wish I could talk Spanish."

The coffee was good and we drank it out of big bowls. The girl brought in a glass dish of raspberry jam.

"Thank you."

"Hey! That's not the way," Bill said. "Say something ironical. Make some crack about Primo de Rivera."

"I could ask her what kind of jam they think they've gotten into in the Riff."

"Poor," said Bill. "Very poor. You can't do it. That's all.

You don't understand irony. You have no pity. Say something pitiful."

"Robert Cohn."

"Not so bad. That's better. Now why is Cohn pitiful? Be ironic."

He took a big gulp of coffee.

"Aw, hell!" I said. "It's too early in the morning."

"There you go. And you claim you want to be a writer, too. You're only a newspaper man. An expatriated newspaper man. You ought to be ironical the minute you get out of bed. You ought to wake up with your mouth full of pity."

—Ernest Hemingway, *The Sun Also Rises* (1926)

1954

When the radio sitcom *Father Knows Best?* moves to television, its sponsor, Kent cigarettes, insists on dropping the question mark, thereby eliminating all the irony and most of the humor.

1957

In his book *Anatomy of Criticism,* Northrop Frye declares irony a major narrative mode, defining it in terms of the relationship between a superior reader and a helpless character suffering life's unfathomable absurdities, a view of irony epitomized in the works of Franz Kafka.

> Irony and humor were not conspicuous in the 1950s. . . . I was in my lawyer's office to sign some contract and a lawyer in the next office was asked to come in and notarize my signature. While he was stamping pages, I continued a discussion with my lawyer about the Broadway theatre, which I said was corrupt; the art of theatre had been totally displaced by the bottom line, all that mattered any more. Looking up at me, the notarizing lawyer said, "That's a communist position, you know." I started to laugh until I saw the constraint in my lawyer's face, and I quickly sobered up.
>
> —Arthur Miller, "Are You Now or Were You Ever?" *The Guardian*, June 16, 2000

1964

Stanley Kubrick's cold war satire *Dr. Strangelove or: How I Learned to Stop Worrying and Love the Bomb* treats the nuclear standoff between the United States and the Soviet Union with such black irony as: "Now I'm not saying we wouldn't get our hair mussed, but I am saying no more than ten to twenty million killed. Tops!" and "You can't fight in here—this is the War Room!" The film opens with an instrumental version of

"Try a Little Tenderness" playing over aerial refueling shots of a B-52 bomber, and ends with a series of nuclear explosions accompanied by Vera Lynn's recording of "We'll Meet Again."

Bonus irony: Slim Pickens, in the role of B-52 bomber pilot Major T. J. Kong, who ends the picture riding a hydrogen bomb like a bucking bull, was never told that the film was a comedy and played the character straight.

> There is no definitive milestone with which we can mark the ushering in of the Age of Irony.
>
> In truth, it's been creeping in stealthily since the mid-1960s. As America lost its starry-eyed faith (aided in part by the Vietnam War and Watergate) in politics, it began to cast a doubtful eye toward other sectors of society. By the time we reached the '80s and, along with it, the Iran-Contra affair, junk bonds, and an increasing fascination with lurid celebrity gossip, nothing was sacred.
>
> —Rachel Leibrock, "Glib Is Out, Sincere Is In—The Age of Irony Is Waning, So Mean What You Say," *Seattle Post-Intelligencer,* February 2, 2001

1970

D. C. Muecke publishes *Irony,* proclaiming irony a "phenomenon of very considerable cultural and literary importance."

1974

University of Chicago literary critic Wayne C. Booth publishes *A Rhetoric of Irony.* Though he acknowledges the "ironic trap" of trying to define "a term that will not stay defined," Booth proposes an elaborate framework of irony and introduces the terms "stable irony" and "unreliable narrator." The book declares irony essential to literature, and its appreciation central to intelligent reading: "Every good reader must be, among other things, sensitive in detecting and reconstructing ironic meanings. . . . Every reader learns that some statements cannot be understood without rejecting what they seem to say." *A Rhetoric of Irony* will be translated into multiple languages and become required reading at many universities.

1978

Randy Newman's hit single "Short People," a satiric commentary on prejudice, provokes controversy. Groups of literal-minded short people organize protests, Newman is denounced from pulpits and even receives death threats. His explanation, that he intended to expose all prejudice by choosing an absurd target—that is, he was being *ironic*—does not placate critics, who accuse him of lying about his motives. Some even suggest that he only *thought* he meant the lyrics ironically and the song revealed true feelings hidden even from himself.

Bonus irony: Randy Newman, a singer/songwriter/composer acclaimed for his sublime lyrics and enlightened point of view, the author of such postmodern classics as "Sail Away," "Political Science," and "I Think It's Going to Rain Today," will probably be best remembered for a lightweight ditty regarded by many as a slur.

"It was too bad that was my one big hit," he says, "a novelty record like the Chipmunks did."

1979

Publication of the revisionist *Testimony: The Memoirs of Shostakovitch,* "related to and edited by" Solomon Volkov, causes a sensation by portraying the Russian composer Dmitry Shostakovich (1906–1975), whom *Pravda* once anointed a "loyal son of the Communist Party," as a "conscientious ironist" whose music was a subtle subversion of the Soviet state.

1986

Kurt Andersen, E. Graydon Carter, and Tom Phillips found *Spy,* a satirical monthly for the Age of Irony. *Spy* would continue to be published until 1998.

1991

An *Esquire* cover story, "Forget Irony—Have a Nice Decade!" ironically proclaims "the New Sincerity," as evidenced by the choice of Jay Leno over David Letterman to succeed Johnny Carson as *Tonight Show* host.

1992

Jungian therapist Evangeline Kane proposes that violent criminals display an inability to understand the multivalent nature of words and therefore don't appreciate such concepts as irony and rhetorical overstatement, which makes them think other people are constantly playing verbal tricks on them, which in turn fuels their rage.

Robert Altman's Hollywood satire *The Player* features dozens of movie stars in auto-ironic cameos, that is, playing themselves as narcissistic, clueless celebrities in order to show that they aren't narcissistic, clueless celebrities.

1993

In a bold effort to improve a flagging professional image, the Teachers for a Democratic Culture ironically try to outlaw irony:

The lesson is clear. Employing irony, speaking tongue in cheek, talking wryly or self-mockingly—these smartass intellectual practices give our whole profession a bad name. If there's one thing calculated to alienate an otherwise friendly and helpful press, it's irony. As Dan Quayle once put it, irony is an ill wind that bites the hand that feeds our fashionable cynicism.

We cannot mince words about irony. Knock it off, and knock it off now. In the first place, nobody understands your little ironies but you and your theorymongering friends. In the second place, even if someone *does* understand your ironies, they still won't translate into newsprint and you'll wind up looking foolish anyway. In the third place, great literature demands of us high seriousness of purpose—not disrespectful laughter and clowning around. So just wipe that smirk off your face.

—M. Berubé and G. Graff, "Regulations for Literary Criticism in the 1990s," *Democratic Culture*

Writing in *The Review of Contemporary Fiction*, David Foster Wallace decries irony as "an agent of a great despair and stasis in U.S. culture," but admits liking it anyway.

1994

Canadian literary scholar Linda Hutcheon publishes *Irony's Edge: The Theory and Politics of Irony*, the first comprehensive study of the subject since Booth's *A Rhetoric of Irony* in 1974. Irony's "evaluative edge," Hutcheon argues, emerges from a shared cultural context, and irony is not merely a trope employed by an "ironist," but a "complex communicative process" in which the *interpreter* of irony is the one who "ironizes."

In the Generation X comedy *Reality Bites,* Winona Ryder flunks a job interview because she can't define "irony." ("But I know it when I see it!" she protests.) Ryder later asks her boyfriend, played by Ethan Hawke, to define the word. "It's when the actual meaning is the complete opposite of the literal meaning," he says.

Release of the "ironic cover" CD *If I Were a Carpenter,* with new renditions of old Carpenters songs performed by the Cranberries, Cracker, Sonic Youth, and Sheryl Crow. Fans of the Carpenters, a mawkish but popular act at a time when hard rock and Motown dominated pop charts, are split: Some embrace the new CD as a fitting tribute; others dismiss it as a travesty. Those who hated the Carpenters tend to like the CD.

1996

Contrary to previous data suggesting that appreciation of linguistic irony develops late in the process of language acquisition, a Boston College study finds that children's sensitivity to rhetorical irony emerges between the ages of five and six.

In his book, *The Comedian as Confidence Man: Studies in Irony Fatigue,* Will Kaufman, a lecturer at the University of Central

Lancashire, coins the term "irony fatigue" to describe the humorist's internal conflict between the social critic who demands to be taken seriously and the joker who never can be. The term will be hijacked to characterize the backlash against facile irony.

Alanis Morissette's "Ironic," in which situations purporting to be ironic are merely sad, random, or annoying (a traffic jam when you're late, a no-smoking sign on your cigarette break) perpetuates widespread misuse of the word and outrages irony prescriptivists. It is of course ironic that "Ironic" is an unironic song about irony. Bonus irony: "Ironic" is widely cited as an example of how Americans don't *get* irony, despite the fact that Alanis Morissette is Canadian.

1998

After a nine-season run and weeks of anticipation, *Seinfeld,* one of the most popular sitcoms in television history, airs its series finale. The episode, written and produced by Larry David, garners 76 million viewers and $4 million per commercial minute, and is hailed as a pop-culture milestone. (One sitcom scholar describes it as a made-for-television "unifying national moment.")

After witnessing a carjacking in a small New England town, the Seinfeld Four (Jerry, George, Kramer, and Elaine) are prosecuted for "criminal indifference" under a local Good Samaritan law. Characters from past episodes testify against them, and they're ultimately convicted of being "indifferent to everything good and decent" and sentenced to a year in jail. Which doesn't seem to faze them: Rather than show remorse, they worry about how they'll look in prison uniforms. That is, they're still the same shallow, narcissistic twits.

> *Seinfeld* finished by destroying its central premise that it was a show about nothing. Instead, it became about something—about the nature of the sitcom and sitcom characters, articulated in a manner that afforded the audience the pleasure of recognition of extra-, intra-, and intertextual references but none of the pleasure of a happy ending. Ironically, many viewers whose enjoyment had come from recognizing the disruptions of narrative conventions were dismayed by the fact that the final episode refused to provide conventional narrative closure.
>
> —Joanne Morreale, "Sitcoms Say Goodbye: The Cultural Spectacle of Seinfeld's Last Episode," *Journal of Popular Film and Television*, fall 2000

John Waters's movie *Pecker* ends with an ironic toast to "the death of irony."

A study reported in the *Journal of Cognitive Psychotherapy* found a schizophrenic group more likely to take ironic utterances literally than did a control group.

The Minnesota Vikings lose to the Atlanta Falcons after Vikings kicker Gary Anderson, who had made forty-six consecutive field goals, misses one in overtime. Asked if he thinks the miss is "ironic," Vikings coach Dennis Green replies, "I don't believe in irony. Things happen. It's part of the game."

University of Edinburgh undergraduate Richard South, twenty-one, receives a high mark for a spoof essay citing bogus texts and phony theories in an attempt to prove that modern university English Literature courses are filled with pretentious nonsense. His facetious answer to the essay question, "Is it valid to read literature historically?" quotes such imaginary authorities as *Art Banditry* and *Rectus Historicus,* and includes such dubious insights as "the only thing a man needs to read a book is glasses." The English department insists it knew the essay was a spoof and marked it on its own terms. Lecturer James Loxley says he did not believe the marker could have been fooled by such a clearly ludicrous answer and adds: "The marker enjoyed the wit and invention of it and gave reward accordingly . . . clearly the marker's comments were equally ironic. One of the fundamental figurative quirks of language is irony—saying what you mean by saying what you don't mean—and this exam was dedicated to exploring that premise." But Mr. South is unconvinced: "High-brow efforts to pass off the marker's reaction to my script as knowing irony are even more implausible than the fantasy sources themselves," he says.

Bonus irony: Department head Cairns Craig warns others not to try the same trick: "Students will not be able to go into exams thinking they can pass by feats of creative imagination."

"Irony is now embedded in the language, ubiquitous and invisible," proclaims Kurt Andersen's millennial comedy of manners, *Turn of the Century.*

Twenty-four-year-old Jedediah Purdy publishes *For Common Things: Irony, Trust, and Commitment in America Today,* an indictment of the "despairing irony" plaguing America. According to Purdy, "unchecked and unchallenged" irony is crippling our young people and rendering our political process impotent. The "ironic temperament" desensitizes us to genuine emotion and ultimately makes us bad citizens. The world no longer interests us, Purdy argues, because we are all "exquisitely self-aware." We enjoy no intimacy, empathy, or affection that has not been "pronounced on a thirty-foot screen before an audience of hundreds." We can't speak of "atonement" or "apology" without knowing that those words "have been put to cynical, almost morally pornographic use by politicians." Purdy finds "something fearful" in what he calls "today's ironic manner." It is, he writes, "a fear of betrayal, disappointment, and humiliation."

Jedediah Purdy was raised on a farm in West Virginia by ruralist parents who moved there, according to Purdy's father, to "pick out a small corner of the world and make it as sane as possible." Home-schooled until he entered Phillips Exeter Academy at the age of sixteen, Purdy graduated from Harvard University and Yale Law School.

This pop-culture bubble boy, having been insulated from what he terms "the subtle codes and taboos of teen culture," was horrified when, as a Harvard freshman, he witnessed fellow students making fun of *Love Story,* a 1970 film in which the beautiful young heroine dies of cancer. ("YOU'RE GONNA DIE!" they shout at Ali MacGraw.) There had been no such ironic TV viewing in his experience—indeed, there had been no TV. Purdy fired off a letter to the *Harvard Crimson* denouncing the ritual as a "cold, self-satisfied . . . hideous practice" and began thinking about writing a book.

The book, *For Common Things: Irony, Trust, and Commitment in America Today,* becomes a cause célèbre and a litmus test, with reviews ranging from rapturous to vitriolic. Purdy is either a twenty-first-century Thoreau, or a "cornpone prophet." *The New York Times* commends him for grappling with the "disease of irony" and anoints him avatar of "The New Sincerity." *Time*'s Walter Kirn pronounces Purdy a "brainy nature boy . . . eloquent beyond his years," and calls the book an "unfashionably passionate attack on the dangers of modern passionlessness."

But *The New York Observer* finds the book "bloated with bombast," and *Harper's* accuses Purdy of promoting "unctuous sentimentality." *Salon* calls Purdy's arguments "intellectual fogy porn," and the *Vancouver Sun* attacks his "sanctimonious naïveté," comparing him to "a Tibetan monk lecturing about wife swapping." Many of the negative reviews are either obtuse or outright dishonest, ignoring Purdy's distinction between positive and negative irony. The *San Francisco Examiner* actually faults Purdy for using the word *jejune.*

Bonus irony 1: Purdy is unfairly attacked by critics who apparently misunderstand (or haven't read) the book. In an afterword to the paperback edition published in 2000, Purdy tries to clarify: "Where I discuss irony in the book, I mean something specific—the contemporary attitude of wry detachment that avoids taking anyone or anything all that seriously, and easily devolves into a meretricious sarcasm. . . . It is a dogmatic skepticism, a stance that dismisses without thought or examination."

Bonus irony 2: Purdy's book generates the kind of unironic, engagé debate it finds lacking in American society.

Bonus irony 3: Through no fault of his own, Purdy becomes the kind of celebrity he decries.

2000

Douglas Coupland proposes a bumper sticker: HONK IF YOU KNOW THE DIFFERENCE BETWEEN IRONY AND SARCASM.

David Gates's *Newsweek* article, "Will We Ever Get Over Irony?" traces the irony backlash to 1926.

2001

James W. Fernandez and Mary Taylor Huber publish *Irony in Action: Anthropology, Practice, and the Moral Imagination,* an examination of irony from an anthropological perspective.

2002

Paul Krassner releases the comedy CD *Irony Lives!* (renamed from its pre-9/11 title, *The Devil in Me*).

Bumper sticker sighted in Santa Monica, California: MY CHILD WAS VOTED "MOST IRONIC STUDENT" AT CROSSROADS SCHOOL.

2003

Italian Prime Minister Silvio Berlusconi sparks controversy in the European Parliament when, in response to questioning from German socialist member Martin Schulz about Berlusconi's use of Italian immunity laws to avoid bribery prosecution, Berlusconi says: "In Italy they are making a movie on Nazi concentration camps. I will propose you for the role of capo." Despite an official rebuke from Parliament, Berlusconi refuses to withdraw the remark, saying that it was meant as a joke inspired by the German legislator's "tone and gestures." "My joke wasn't meant to be offensive," Berlusconi maintains. "It was an ironic joke, perhaps the translation wasn't done in an ironic sense."

Self-described "ironic-therapist" Dr. Liz Margoshes tells *The Village Voice* that ironic people have special needs, therapy-wise:

Ironic people often have trouble with the hyper-earnestness of traditional therapists. And they really don't want their slant toward the world analyzed away as a defense.

Irony is a particularly *useful* stance in therapy. Seeing the world with ironic detachment is similar to what the Buddhists tell us to work toward—a giving up of attachments or rigid beliefs that get in the way of directly experiencing the world. Irony is a wonderful tool for examining things. You can stand back and watch yourself feel and think. Gradually you change from believing that there is an "objective," immutable "reality" ("I'm shy," "Men don't like me," "I'll never get out of this dead-end job," etc.) to seeing how your beliefs and attitudes are really just thoughts—and thoughts can be changed—and that it's actually your own subjectivity that's getting in your way! Once you see that, you start to see that actually there are no limits to what you can think, feel, and do.

—Dr. Liz Margoshes, quoted by Elizabeth Zimmer, "New Stances Sharpen Traditional Disciplines," *The Village Voice*, September 17–23, 2003

2004

Ironycorner, a store with nothing but articles of clothing bearing the word IRONY, opens in Tokyo.

In a *60 Minutes* interview with Ed Bradley, Bob Dylan, whose poetic lyrics galvanized a generation of social activists, claims he was misunderstood:

Dylan: My stuff were songs, you know? They weren't sermons. If you examine the songs, I don't believe you're gonna find anything in there that says that I'm a spokesman for anybody or anything really.

Bradley: But they saw it.

Dylan: They must not have heard the songs.

Bradley: It's ironic, that the way that people viewed you was just the polar opposite of the way you viewed yourself.

Dylan: Isn't that something?

Tom Wolfe's novel *I Am Charlotte Simmons* receives the Bad Sex in Fiction award from Britain's *Literary Review,* whose judges cite the following excerpt as a sample of Wolfe's "ghastly and boring" prose:

Slither slither slither slither went the tongue. But the hand, that was what she tried to concentrate on, the hand, since it has the entire terrain of her torso to explore and not just the otorhinolaryngological caverns—oh God, it was not just at the border where the flesh of the breast joins the pectoral sheath of the

chest—no, the hand was cupping her entire right—
Now!

Wolfe protests that the passage was meant to be ironic, citing his use of the word *otorhinolaryngological*: "I purposely chose the most difficult scientific word I could to show this is not an erotic scene," he explains. "There's nothing like a nine-syllable word to chase Eros off the premises."

2005

When JetBlue Flight 292 from Burbank to JFK develops landing gear trouble after takeoff, the Airbus A320 with 145 people aboard circles LAX to burn fuel before attempting an emergency landing. Television networks abandon regular programming to cover the unfolding drama, and passengers watch the live video on in-flight TV. After a safe landing, passenger Alexandra Jacobs tells reporters: "We couldn't believe the irony that we might be watching our own demise on television—it was all too post-post-modern."

Concerned over low turnout in elections, especially among young voters, the European Parliament launches a Web site featuring "citizen friendly" information and self-effacingly "ironic" marketing, including T-shirts poking fun at the parliament's arcane legislative procedures.

2006

David Friedman's ironicsans.com begins offering "pre-pixelated" clothes.

I ♥ IRONY bumper sticker sighted in Branson, Missouri. Bonus irony: I ♥ IRONY bumper sticker sighted in Branson, Missouri.

Irony Takes a Holiday

> Life does not cease to be funny when people die any more than it ceases to be serious when we laugh.
> —George Bernard Shaw, *The Doctor's Dilemma* (1911)

During the dark days after the 9/11 attacks, in a climate of heightened national unity, when Americans were telling each other that "everything has changed," culture commentators announced the death of irony.

There had been irony backlashes before, but nothing like this. *Vanity Fair* editor Graydon Carter, cofounder of the ultraironic *Spy* magazine, proclaimed a "new era of earnestness": "I have a feeling something fresh will emerge, the way people think, the way people create, is going to change," he wrote. *Time* magazine essayist Roger Rosenblatt announced the "end of the age of irony" and predicted we would no longer "fail to take things seriously." The historian Taylor Branch told the *Los Angeles Times* that the attacks were a "turning point against a generation of cynicism for all of us," and George Schlatter, producer of the 1960s hit *Laugh-In,* told *The Christian Science Monitor,* "This may be an event which historians look back to as the beginning of a new era of sensitivity, introspection, and growth."

The deadpan fake newspaper *The Onion* suspended publication, and *The New Yorker* omitted cartoons. George Carlin changed the title of his HBO special from *I Kinda Like It When a Lotta People Die* to *Complaints and Grievances,* and Courtney Love announced plans to enlist in the Marines and buy stock in American companies. (Both the Marines and the market declined.) Several Hollywood films were withdrawn from distribution because they dealt with terrorism, including the Arnold Schwarzenegger vehicle *Collateral Damage.* Broadway attendance plummeted and theaters went dark. CBS postponed the Emmy Awards show, and the four networks aired a star-studded telethon for 9/11 victims. On *The Tonight Show,* Jay Leno declared, "Bush is smart now."

On his first show after the attacks, David Letterman dispensed with an opening monologue and welled up as he wondered aloud whether it was right to do a show so soon. Later, comforting a weeping Dan Rather, Letterman broke into tears himself. "It's terribly sad here in New York City," he said. "There is only one requirement for any of us, and that's to be courageous."

Writing in *GQ,* Joe Queenan declared Letterman's teary performance a turning point:

By expressing his unquestionably heartfelt sentiments in a direct and touching fashion, the man who had done more than any other American to elevate irony to a viable urban lifestyle signaled to his colleagues, imitators, and perhaps even Paul Shaffer that the time of sneering detachment had come to an end.

—Joe Queenan, "Unemployment Among Ironists Rose 65% Last Month," GQ, December 2001

But the Post-Ironic Age never dawned, the New Earnestness failed to take hold, and dissenting voices soon chimed in. *New York* magazine editor Mark Horowitz answered Graydon Carter: "I think it's especially funny that the editors of *Vanity Fair* have become the new imams, spouting moral seriousness and declaring that all frivolity must come to an end. If tourism, real estate, and finance in N.Y. collapse, then people will really be earnest and serious. If we lose our frivolity, that really is a victory for terrorists."

Jedediah Purdy, who condemned the spread of cynical irony in his 1999 book, *For Common Things: Irony, Trust, and Commitment in America Today,* called for a new kind of irony "to keep dangerous excesses of passion and self-righteousness and extreme conviction at bay," that is, to combat the kind of fanaticism that motivated the terrorists. David Beers, writing in Salon.com ("Irony Is Dead! Long Live Irony!"), called for an "engaged" irony, while pointing out the irony of abandoning a "cleareyed" ironic sensibility just when we need it most to avoid being swept up in "the new jingoism." National Public Radio essayist Ralph Schoenstein quipped that the death of irony was about as likely as the death of stupidity. And two weeks after the attacks, *The Onion* returned with such headlines as:

U.S. VOWS TO DEFEAT WHOEVER IT IS WE'RE AT WAR WITH

AMERICAN LIFE TURNS INTO BAD JERRY BRUCKHEIMER MOVIE

BUSH SR. APOLOGIZES TO SON FOR FUNDING BIN LADEN IN '80S

The same *Onion* issue ran the following item:

REPORT: GEN X IRONY, CYNICISM MAY BE PERMANENTLY OBSOLETE

Austin, TX—According to Generation X sources, the recent attack on America may have rendered cynicism and irony permanently obsolete. "Remember the day after the attack, when all the senators were singing 'God Bless America,' arm-in-arm?" asked Dave Holt, twenty-nine. "Normally, I'd make some sarcastic wisecrack about something like that. But this time, I was deeply moved." Added Holt: "This earnestness can't last forever. Can it?"

In an interview with the *San Francisco Chronicle, Onion* senior editor Carol Kolb defended the return to irreverence: "No one at *The Onion* believes that irony is obsolete," she said.

"Irony, if used correctly, is criticism, and a legitimate way to comment on the news."

The New Yorker ran a cartoon with the caption, "It's hard, but I'm slowly getting back to hating everyone," and the magazine's cartoon editor, Robert Mankoff, declared that after the attacks, humor became "hyper-ironic": "With the Office of Homeland Security and all the [security alert] color codes, it became something you couldn't help but make fun of," Mankoff said. "You have an Office of Homeland Security to make us think we have security and in reality we don't know what we're doing—now that's ironic."

On September 29, New York mayor Rudolph Giuliani appeared on *Saturday Night Live*. Asked by the show's executive producer Lorne Michaels, "Can we be funny?" Giuliani replied, "Why start now?"

And in a radio interview with Kurt Andersen, the novelist John Barth tried to put the issue in historical perspective:

I don't believe for a moment, as some op-ed piece said, that in the wake of 9/11 irony is a kind of obscenity. That's like the old argument that we heard after the Second World War—that after the Holocaust art is irrelevant. And we know where that sentiment is coming from; one honors the horror that produced that sentiment. But it ain't so. And, indeed, we think . . . of the classic New Orleans funerals where the band played a nice blues on the way to the cemetery and then an up-tempo lively number on the way home. . . . They honor the fact of death on the way out and they celebrate and affirm the fact of life. So I think it's probably not only permissible, I hope, to write comedy in the wake of 9/11—it's probably almost necessary.

—John Barth, Public Radio International, *Studio 360,*
    December 15, 2001

Postscript: In June of 2002, Graydon Carter recanted: "I've said stupider things, they just haven't been picked up," he told the *San Francisco Chronicle,* then issued an ironic retraction to *The Washington Post:* "I meant to say IRONING is dead—not irony, IRONING."

Irony in Action

IRONIC WORDS AND PHRASES

Eirōnia, the Greek root of *irony,* derives from the verb "to speak," but words are not ironic per se. Context is all. Writer and reader (or speaker and listener) create irony together, out of what literary scholar Linda Hutcheon calls "perceived disjunctions." If someone ironizes in the forest with no one else there to perceive it, no irony happens. So, for example, false courtesy, that is, when someone says "Have a nice day," but really means, "I hope you get cancer," qualifies as irony only when the target or a knowing observer is aware of the ironist's ill will.

At any given time and place—early twenty-first-century America, say—certain words and phrases are intrinsically ironic because of their cultural connotations. "The sounds of silence," "a definite maybe," and "not that there's anything wrong with that" are all, well, *straightforwardly* ironic. Everybody knows that "It's not that I don't trust you . . ." means, "I don't trust you."

But there are less obvious cases. "Your friend," for example, is ironic 75 percent of the time, according to Kurt Andersen's novel, *Turn of the Century.* It gets tricky. Fortunately, we have guidance from an irony maven:

A Survey of Words That Can Only Be Used 100% Ironically

Helpful Criteria: Might Sammy have used this word to greet Dean Martin on a stage?

Might this word have been used by *TV Guide* to describe Marlo Thomas at some point during the run of *That Girl*?

Might I hear this word barked at a stranger from a Rancho Mirage golf cart? Might I read this word on the box liner of a VHS cassette titled *Teenage Panty Party*? Might Kraft use this word to describe one of their many fine dairy-related products? Could anyone under thirty-five say this word with a straight face?

The List

Cabaret, cheesy, cocktail, co-ed, coiffure, cosmic, country club, crusty, cultural elite, daddy-o, daffy, dame, dreamy, energy, entertainer, excellent, extra chunky, fabulous, family values, flavor crystals, food chain, Frank, Frisco, groovy, highball, hip, homemaker, honey, hot, hubby, humanitarian, hunk, instant, kicky, kooky, little women, -Lite, madcap, Madison Avenue, mentholated, modern, moi, new, nugget, nutty, o', perky, prom, pulsating, queer, ritzy, real, runner-up, sexy, show tunes, splitsville, spouse, swanky, swinging, swingingest, tasty, the wife, thrusting, treat, Vegas.

Bonus words: Words perilously close to becoming 100 percent ironic: pain, share, them, they.

—Douglas Coupland, *The New Republic,* November 11, 1992

Just as there are degrees in the quality of irony, from the polemical thunder of Jonathan Swift to the pale, seemingly pointless irony of Wes Anderson, there are also gradations in the way irony is characterized, and deft use of irony modifiers is the mark of the master. To paraphrase Mark Twain, the difference between the almost right irony modifier and the right irony modifier is like the difference between lightning and the lightning bug.

Irony can be *delicate, gentle, nice, sweet, lovely, silky, delicious, exquisite, luminous, divine, rich, profound, grand, powerful, monumental, supreme, crowning, mythic, perfect,* or *final.* It can be *unfortunate, terrible, grim, dark, grave, harsh, brutal, cruel, bitter, acute, pointed, painful, excruciating, intolerable, bizarre, grotesque,* or just plain *strange.* Irony can be *apparent, obvious, palpable, fundamental, central, abiding,* or *enduring;* it can be *comic* or *tragic, giddy* or *sobering, smirking, deadpan, sly,* or *wry* (though *wry irony* borders on redundancy). Irony can *disconcert, unsettle, boggle, twist, hover,* or form a *halo.* It can be enlisted as a reproach when termed *self-referential, self-reflexive,* or *self-serving,* deployed as a *defensive, preemptive,* or *self-protective wall,* or marshaled to *cripple, wither, savage, sting, cut,* or *bite.*

Irony comes in varying quantities, from a *touch,* a *hint,* a *trace,* or a *whiff* to a *rich lode* or *irony aplenty.* A particularly ironic situation can be *rife with irony, brimming with irony, dripping with irony, saturated with irony, drenched in irony, swimming in irony, irony-soaked, irony-suffused, coated with irony,* or *irony-caked.* Too much of it, however, and you risk being *cankered with* or *entombed in* irony. *No small irony* is an ironic way of describing a big irony. *Irony of ironies* is as ironic as it gets.

Use of *'n'* is a quick 'n' easy way to register irony, as are the suffixes *o-matic* and *o-rama.* Well, *so to speak,* and *as it were* are also used ironically to flag an intentional pun.

IRONIC PUNCTUATION

In printed or written text or in speech, quotation marks not only allow you to distance yourself from what you're writing or saying, they're also useful when you want to signal that you're being ironic, as when, for example, you suspect that your audience is irony challenged. But be advised: Whether written or spoken, quotation marks can get out of hand, as in the case of a former neighbor of mine who, during a power outage on our block, told me, and I quote: "I just spoke to the— quote—*power company,* who said the—quote—*electricity* will be back on by—quote—*six o'clock.*" Maybe the poor guy had a verbal tic, but then again, maybe it's a—quote—*slippery slope,* so be careful.

The young reporters . . . press on. Working with Garry
Marshall and Daryl Hannah, how was that?

"Well, I feel that they're very lucky to be working with
me, let's be honest," Mr. Piven says, aware of the print
reporter at his shoulder. "That's irony. Irony doesn't
print." He repeats it. "Irony doesn't print. It only works in
this medium. So I'm winning here, losing there." He
points back and forth, from them to the reporter.
"WINNN-ing. LOOOS-ing."

> —Jeremy Piven, quoted by Joyce Wadler, "A Night Out
> With: Jeremy Piven, Embracing Irony," *The New York Times*,
> May 7, 2006

Occasionally you can almost *hear* the quotes around a word
or phrase. This powerful technique, known as *speaking in italics,*
produces what might be called *audible quotation marks.* Exaggerated syllabication—slowing down and emphasizing a word, or
even adding an extra syllable—can also be ironic, as in the case
of *ex cah lusive,* for example. Clearing the throat (*ahem . . .*) or
pausing before a word or phrase is usually sufficient to indicate
irony, but prefacing a remark with "ironically" or "ironically
enough" is like elbowing the listener in the ribs or laughing at
your own joke.

Deliberate overuse of exclamation points can be ironic, but
the technique flirts with the sophomoric and thus requires the
reader's knowledge that the writer is not an idiot.

The term "Verbal Irony" is unsatisfactory since the ironist may use other media. One can bow or smile ironically, paint ironical pictures, or compose ironical music. But since the aim of all "Behavioral Irony," whatever medium is employed, is to convey a meaning, this kind of irony is still to be regarded as "linguistic."

—D. C. Muecke, *Irony* (1970)

IRONIC NAMES

Names and naming are fertile ground for irony: American football involves little kicking. Greenland is covered by ice. A white man named Paul Whiteman (1890–1967) was the first popularizer of a black art form called jazz. Jaime Sin (1928–2004) was a Catholic cardinal and key figure in the "people power" revolt that ousted Philippine dictator Ferdinand Marcos (let's say it together: *Cardinal Sin*). A young actor named Krishna Bhanji changed his name in order to get English-speaking roles but eventually came full circle and played Gandhi . . . as "Ben Kingsley."

Marketeers are notorious for ironic naming. The names of sport utility vehicles, for example, are almost always ironic, given that fewer than ten percent of them ever leave asphalt. Hence, Explorer, Expedition, Navigator, Mountaineer, Pathfinder, Blazer, Denali, Yukon, Durango:

The other day, I saw an acquaintance of mine in a boxy
steed called a Durango. Say it out loud for me:
"Durango." Can you get the syllables off your tongue
without irony? In the post-*Seinfeld* era, can anyone say
"Durango" without giving it an Elaine Benes enunciation
at every syllable? Doo-RANG-Go.

The true irony comes from the fact that this
thoroughly market-researched word no longer has any
core meaning. No one comprehends its denotation
(Colorado town) but only its vague connotations
(rugged individualism, mastery over the wilderness,
cowboy endurance). The word does not pin down
meaning so much as conjure up images.

—Jack Hitt, "The Hidden Life of SUVs," *Mother Jones,*
     July/August 1999

Pointedly ironic naming can be a political tool, from
Hoovervilles, the encampments of poor and homeless that
sprang up during Herbert Hoover's presidency, to Ladyfest, an
annual nonprofit feminist event featuring performances, panels,
and workshops designed to promote the "artistic and political
lives of women":

In addition to fostering a can-do attitude, Ladyfest
draws upon an irreverence for traditional feminism and
language, as evidenced by its name. The use of "lady"
is full of irony, a tongue-in-cheek undercutting of the

dainty, moneyed sound of the word with the image of
women rebels.

> —Noy Thrupkaew, "Ladies, Please: Cavorting with the Very
> Latest Punk Feminists at Ladyfest D.C. 20002," the American
> Prospect Online, August 9, 2002

Rap names are often ironic. Sean Combs's succession of
self-conferred nicknames (Puff Daddy, P. Diddy, Puffy, Diddy)
may appeal to fans but seem self-parodic if not downright ludicrous to casual observers. (Likewise Ludacris, formerly
known as Chris Lova Lova, né Christopher Brian Bridges.)

The irony of some names depends on who's using them:

Canuck (n.)

To some the noun means simply "a Canadian, a citizen
of Canada," about on par with *Yankee* as a name for a
U.S. citizen—slang or conversational at worst, and
certainly nondisparaging. To others it means "a French-
Canadian," and some people consider it an ethnic slur
and therefore taboo. The Separatist movement in
Quebec embroils the word in quarrels of language,
religion, and nationalistic politics; it can be explosive.
And some think it ironic that the western provinces are
proud of the Vancouver *Canucks,* a National Hockey
League team, while Quebec's Montreal NHL team bears
the all-Canadian name of *Maple Leafs.* Be wary of using
Canuck in other than hockey contexts; many Canadians

find it offensive when applied to them by outsiders, even though they may use it of themselves.

—Kenneth G. Wilson, *The Columbia Guide to Standard American English* (1993)

GESTURAL IRONY

Irony inhabits all forms of communication, not just verbal, and there are various forms of gestural or behavioral irony. "Air quotes," for example, curling the fingers in the air in the shape of quotation marks while speaking a word or phrase are a, well, *handy* way to signify irony. In a classic *Saturday Night Live* sketch, Chris Farley uses them to explain why he failed an audition for a TV news anchor job: "I guess I just wasn't [air quotes] *photogenic*; I guess I don't have [air quotes] *classic good looks.*"

Other behavioral intimations of irony include winks, nudges, raised eyebrows, or a smile when your heart is aching. In an episode of *The Wild Wild West* (1965–1970), Artemus Gordon (Ross Martin) pretends to wink in order to fool an army officer into expecting a bribe. The wink says, "Play along and I'll take care of you later." But Gordon has no intention of delivering on the promise—to reward the officer would be to foil the plan. Yet to openly renege would also bring disaster. So, when it's time to pay up, Gordon winks repeatedly, slyly indicating that what the officer interpreted (and Gordon in-

tended him to interpret) as a wink . . . is only an involuntary
tic devoid of hidden meaning. Gordon accomplishes his clever
deception through mendacious irony, or what might be called
"faux irony by conduct."

Daniel Negreanu
(Reuters/Steve Marcus)

[Daniel] Negreanu is one of the most fascinating
examples of the new poker face. During most games,
his face is so confusingly animated—with friendly gibes,
eyebrow arching, snatches of song, and sudden mimic
impulses—that his rare spells of straight-faced
concentration seem like just another ironic stratagem.
    —Kevin Conley, "The Players: A New Generation Makes a Card
        Game a Career Choice," *The New Yorker,* July 11 and 18, 2005

IRONIC ATTIRE

Young people like to dress ironically, and the ironic T-shirt is the quintessential ironic garment, cheap yet highly effective. Bad rock bands are universal fodder for ironic T-shirts. There are regional variations, of course: A Future Farmers of America T-shirt is ironic in approximately half the country, that is, in the big cities and the coastal states, but not in the heartland. A lime green polyester suit is ironic in Manhattan, but not in Tulsa. There's considerable irony in logowear, according to one commentator:

> When you see someone sporting a shirt with the manufacturer's name inscribed in bold letters across the chest, it's hard to ignore the irony. Here the apparel wearer is paying the company to promote its name, rather than vice versa. For the privilege of being a walking billboard, one forks over many times what one would normally pay for the same product. So next time you wear a pair of shoes with that logo, or a pair of pants with some large initials stitched on them, or a shirt with a brightly painted name, remember, you're inadvertently advertising the company. The word "advertise" comes to us from Latin *advertere*, meaning "to turn toward" or "to pay attention." The word "inadvertently" derives from the same source. In

other words, by not paying attention, we *are* paying attention.

—**Anu Garg**, A.Word.A.Day, posted on February 3, 2003, at wordsmith.org/awad

Burberry's signature checked print was briefly de rigueur among trendy young Londoners who wore it as an ironic comment on class stereotypes, but older customers were oblivious to the irony. Hush Puppies were a dying brand until young New Yorkers began wearing them ironically in 1994; now they're sold in malls nationwide. And while young people dress them*selves* ironically, old people dress their *dogs* ironically.

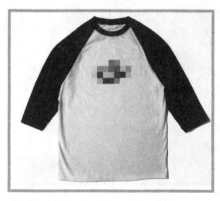

Photo by David Friedman/Ironic Sans (ironicsans.com)

On reality TV shows, recognizable logos on clothing are pixelated to avoid trademark violations, inspiring the blog Ironic Sans to create and market the real thing.

Ironic dressing is probably best left to amateurs. At least two famous designers have incurred the wrath of religious groups for attempts at such cultural irony, as when Karl Lagerfeld dressed Claudia Schiffer in a tight bodice embroidered with verses from the Koran, or when Jean Paul Gaultier created an entire collection of "Hasidic" clothing. In response to criticism, Gaultier explained that he was merely showing appreciation for the "simplicity" of the "Hasidic lifestyle."

Bastions of Irony

With puberty's reverse metamorphosis (that is, butterfly to caterpillar) come greater cognitive abilities and what might be termed the "ironic break": Adolescents go from childlike equanimity to hormone-addled disaffection as it dawns on them that life is not as advertised. They begin to perceive the world's injustices and absurdities, and it hurts. Glib adolescent irony, the fear of looking foolish combined with disdain for anything adult, is the balm, one of the side effects of which is acute embarrassment by parents:

A while ago, *The New York Times* printed an item concerning an eleven-year-old girl who was overheard on the streets of East Hampton, N.Y., telling her father, "Daddy, Daddy, please don't sing!"
The daddy was Billy Joel.

The irony, of course, is that a lot of people would pay BIG money to hear Billy Joel sing. But of course these people are not Billy Joel's offspring. To his daughter, Billy Joel apparently represents the same thing that all parents represent to their preteen offspring: Bozo Rama. At that age, there is nothing in the world more embarrassing than a parent.

—Dave Barry, *The Miami Herald*, August 11, 1996

When you're younger, you think a little irony is all you need. You think it'll get you to the grave, but it won't. Loss always seeps through. You do need to deal with it.

—Douglas Coupland, quoted by Bronwen Hruska, "Is There Life After Irony for Coupland?" *San Francisco Chronicle*, March 1, 1994

CANADA

Canada? Yes and no. Americans tend to think of Canadians (when we think of them at all) as bland and literal-minded. Canadians (many of whom regard Americans as obnoxious and literal-minded) are divided on the question of their own irony, and the evidence is indeed mixed: *Vanity Fair* editor Graydon Carter, who proclaimed the death of irony in the wake of 9/11, is Canadian. So is Alanis Morissette, whose 1993 hit "Ironic" is clueless about irony. Lorne Michaels, the Toronto-born creator and executive producer of *Saturday Night Live,* said of his early days in Canadian television: "The idea of irony—where you say one thing and mean something different, was considered . . . not straightforward."

The irony backlash in Canada was ferocious. Writing in *Maclean's* in 1999, the American-born Canadian humorist Charles Gordon decried a pervading "ironic sensibility" and "empty cleverness that passes for pop culture [in Canada]." And the Canadian short story writer Alice Munro publicly lamented an excess of irony in her early work: "Irony was so big [in Canada] then that it got under your skin and you sort of didn't recognize it," she said in a *New Yorker* interview.

Yet Canada has produced a world-class irony monger in the novelist and social critic Douglas Coupland, along with such gifted practitioners as the comedians Martin Short, Catherine O'Hara, and Eugene Levy. And if academic interest is any measure of a nation's irony quotient, Canadian critic Northrop Frye's *Anatomy of Criticism* (1957) is a major contribution to what might be called "irony studies." The debate is insoluble, of course, so we'll simply give a giant of Canadian letters the last word:

> We are an ironic people; irony and some sourness is mixed in our nature. It is a matter of climate. We are a northern people.
> —Robertson Davies, *Conversations* (1989)

DESPAIR, INC.

A counterinspirational catalog and Web site (despair.com) offering "demotivational" calendars, posters, coffee mugs, and note cards with "positive negations":

MOTIVATION. THE POSITIVELY NEGATIVE WAY.™
HOPE SPRINGS ETERNAL from industries that package and sell it for our consumption. Yet in these troubled times, cynical marketers have begun to fashion negative parodies to soothe the intellects, if not the souls, of a population grown weary of manufactured hope.

  With our Positive Negations™ line, these two worlds collide, as idyllic titles are coupled with dispiriting sayings. The result? A meta-level compound that promises happiness from afar, then slaps you in the face for being so gullible. Très postmodern!

Motivation: If A Pretty Poster and a Cute Saying Are All It Takes to Motivate You, You Probably Have a Very Easy Job. The Kind Robots Will Be Doing Soon.

Success: Some People Dream of Success, While Other People Live to Crush Those Dreams.

Ambition: The Journey of a Thousand Miles Sometimes Ends Very, Very Badly.

ESPN *SPORTSCENTER*

The daily sportscast fairly drips with sportswriterly contempt for everything, and the relentlessly hipper-than-thou 'tude gets old, but the long-running series of commercials for *SportsCenter* featuring the biggest names in sports are consistently funny.

MAD MAGAZINE

The first experience of irony, satire, and parody for generations of preadolescents.

1985 cover showing Alfred E. Neuman crushed to death
beneath a parachuted crate of first-aid supplies
(DC Comics/*MAD* magazine)

NEW YORKER CARTOONS

The New Yorker has done for irony what *Life* did for photography.

By the 1930s and '40s, the *New Yorker* cartoon had adopted two basic modes. First, it made fun of its readers' aspirations—social, intellectual, economic, and romantic—by satirizing their language, their professions, their pastimes, their dress, and their physical mannerisms. This was the humor of self-recognition, but also of self-congratulation, since a fool who can laugh at his folly is not a fool but something rarer and finer: a self-ironist.

—Walter Kirn, "Blame *The New Yorker*," *The New York Times Book Review*, December 26, 2004

Moral self-infatuation has its own corruptions, after all. With time, almost every other principle of the magazine acquired an ironic echo, a sort of cackling aftermath.

—Renata Adler, *Gone: The Last Days of* The New Yorker (2000)

PROFESSIONAL WRESTLING

The deception is transparent, of course, but fans *pretend* to take it seriously:

"Other professional sports are trite now. There's no more Kirby Puckett in baseball, no more Michael Jordan in basketball," offers [college student] Kowalski. "Yeah, wrestling is fixed, but at least there are still superheroes."

—Carolyn Kleiner, *U.S. News & World Report*, May 17, 1999

SEINFELD

The self-described "show about nothing," ostensibly without a moral agenda, whose writers' guiding principle was "no hugging, no learning," may have had substance after all:

I think we could have a healthy debate (maybe over at the *Entertainment Weekly* Web site) as to whether *Seinfeld* is ironic or is in fact an elegantly gloved Jedediah Purdy–esque critique of irony. In fact, the final episode (a much-underrated encapsulation of the show's recurrent themes) has an almost Waughian valence in its savage mockery of the loss of self and soul among the cosmopolite heathen. You'll recall that the four lead characters land in a small New England town where they witness a crime and fail to intervene. They are jailed for violating the town's Good Samaritan law (talk about the commons!), and the show ends with the four of them in a jail cell recapitulating the dialogue from the show's first episode, creating an absurdist Moebius strip of solipsism,

emptiness, and stone-cold loserdom. Is this not like
Tony Last in *A Handful of Dust*, stranded up the Amazon
reading Dickens into eternity for the crazed Mr. Todd?
    —Michael Hirschorn, *Slate*, September 22, 1999

THE SIMPSONS

The Simpsons has more levels than a shopping-mall
parking lot.
    —Jonah Goldberg, *National Review*, April 28, 1999

The animated sitcom about a yellow-skinned cartoon family
(Homer, his wife Marge, and their children Bart, Lisa, and
Maggie) who live in the fictitious town of Springfield, USA, is
the longest-running sitcom in history. Its comedy runs the
gamut from snappy repartee to goofy slapstick, wicked satire to
farce, targeting everything from television itself to the American middle class. (Homer describes his family as "upper lower
middle class.") The densely allusive, obsessively self-referential
half-hour has been the subject of serious academic work, much
of it positive. Paul A. Cantor of the University of Virginia argues that *The Simpsons* is one of the most socially conscious
programs on television because it encourages good parenting
and the nuclear family despite satirizing it. "In effect, the show
says, 'Take the worst case scenario—the Simpsons—and even
that family is better than no family,'" writes Professor Cantor.
Gerry Bowler, professor of philosophy at Canadian Nazarene

College, claims the show promotes religion by taking it seriously enough to make fun of it, noting that in various episodes, "prayer is almost always efficacious," and "God answers his petitioners almost immediately."

But before we spoil *all* the fun, let's look at the "hyper-irony" theory posited by Carl Matheson, head of the Philosophy department at the University of Manitoba, whose book, *The Simpsons and Philosophy: The D'oh! of Homer* (2001) proclaims *The Simpsons* "the deepest show on television," but warns against thinking that it has a moral agenda. On the contrary: It is utterly nihilistic, and thereby accurately reflects American society's lack of a binding ethic, and the show's "hyper-ironic" humor is "based less on a shared sense of humanity than on a sense of world-weary cleverer-than-thouness," Matheson argues. The show promotes nothing, offers no moral lessons, spares nothing and no one. It puts forward positions only to undercut them, without offering something better. According to Matheson, this process of undercutting "runs so deeply that we cannot regard the show as merely cynical; it manages to undercut its cynicism, too."

> *The Simpsons* . . . treats nearly everything as a target,
> every stereotypical character, every foible, and every
> institution. It plays games of one-upmanship with its
> audience members by challenging them to identify the
> avalanche of allusions it throws down to them. . . . I think
> that the thirty seconds or so of apparent redemption in
> each episode of *The Simpsons* is there mainly to allow

us to soldier on for twenty-one and a half minutes of maniacal cruelty at the beginning of the next episode. In other words, the heart-warming family moments help *The Simpsons* to live on as a series. The comedy does not exist for the sake of a message; the occasional illusion of a positive message exists to enable us to tolerate more comedy.

—Carl Matheson, *The Simpsons and Philosophy: The D'oh! of Homer* (2001)

Meta–irony abounds in *The Simpsons*. Nelson's laugh ("HA-HA!") punctuates ironic moments, and there are frequent allusions to both the misuse of the word and the cultural debate over its meaning:

Homer:	How ironic. Now he's blind after a life of enjoying being able to see!
Bart:	Lisa's in trouble. Ha! The ironing is delicious.
Lisa:	The word is *irony*.
Bart:	Huh?
Disaffected youth #1:	Here comes that cannonball guy. He's cool.
Disaffected youth #2:	Are you being sarcastic, dude?
Disaffected youth #1:	I don't even know anymore.

TELEVISION

You watch television, you know it's bad for you, but you can't stop. Solution: Watch *ironically*. According to David Foster Wallace, people love/hate television, so they try to "disinfect themselves . . . by watching TV with weary irony." For William Gibson, watching television ironically is at the core of American culture:

> In our hypermediated age, we have come to suspect that watching television constitutes a species of work. Post-industrial creatures of an information economy, we increasingly sense that accessing media is what we do. We have become terminally self-conscious. There is no such thing as simple entertainment. We watch ourselves watching. We watch ourselves watching Beavis and Butt-Head, who are watching rock videos. Simply to watch, without the buffer of irony in place, might reveal a fatal naïveté.
>
> —William Gibson, "The Net Is a Waste of Time," *The New York Times Magazine,* July 14, 1996

WAR

War is ironic, if not for those on the home front, then for those fighting it:

War is ironic because everybody believes that life is pleasurable, and they should. They have a right to believe that, especially if they're brought up under a Constitution that talks about the pursuit of happiness. To have public life shot through with that kind of optimism and complacency is the grounds for horrible, instructive irony when those generalities prove not true. War tends to prove them not true. War is about survival and it's about mass killing and it's about killing or being killed—that is, in the infantry—and it is extremely unpleasant. One realizes that a terrible mistake has been made somewhere, either by the optimistic eighteenth century or by mechanistic twentieth century. The two don't fit together somehow, and that creates, obviously, irony.

—**Paul Fussell,** quoted by Sheldon Hackney, "A Conversation
    with Paul Fussell," *Humanities,* November/December 1996

YIDDISHKEIT

Yiddishkeit, literally "Jewishness," positively brims with irony:

Customer: Is the soup hot?
Waiter: No, it's cold.

—Overheard at the Stage Delicatessen, New York City, circa
    1960

During a gigantic celebration in Red Square, after Trotsky had been sent into exile, Stalin, on Lenin's great tomb, suddenly and excitedly raised his hand to still the acclamations: "Comrades, comrades! A most historic event! A cablegram—of congratulations—from Trotsky!"

The hordes cheered and chortled and cheered again, and Stalin read the historic cable aloud:

JOSEPH STALIN
KREMLIN, MOSCOW
YOU WERE RIGHT AND I WAS WRONG. YOU ARE THE TRUE HEIR OF LENIN. I SHOULD APOLOGIZE.
TROTSKY

You can imagine what a roar, what an explosion of astonishment and triumph erupted in Red Square now!

But in the front row, below the podium, a little tailor called, "Pst! Pst! Comrade Stalin."

Stalin leaned down.

The tailor said, "Such a message, Comrade Stalin. For the ages! But you read it without the right *feeling*!"

Whereupon Stalin raised his hand and stilled the throng once more. "Comrades! Here is a simple worker, a loyal Communist, who says I didn't read the message from Trotsky with enough feeling! Come, Comrade Worker! Up here! *You* read this historic communication!"

So the little tailor went up to the reviewing stand and took the cablegram from Stalin and read:

JOSEPH STALIN
KREMLIN, MOSCOW
YOU WERE RIGHT AND *I* WAS WRONG? *YOU* ARE THE
TRUE HEIR OF LENIN? *I* SHOULD APOLOGIZE?
TROTSKY!

—**Leo Rosten,** *The Joys of Yiddish* (1968)

Masters of Irony

Irony is a vital presence in the works of great artists, writers, and thinkers, including: Socrates, Sophocles, Aristophanes, Chaucer, Erasmus, Voltaire, Montaigne ("the father of the modern form of ironic skepticism" according to Jedediah Purdy), Cervantes, Benjamin Franklin (the *cool* Founding Father was a crackerjack self-ironist), Flaubert, Kierkegaard, Anatole France, Thomas Hardy, Nietzsche, Dostoevsky, Oscar Wilde, Edith Wharton, O. Henry (in his story "By Courier," a character speaks "in a deliberate sweet voice that seemed to clothe her words in a diaphanous garment of impalpable irony"), Chekhov, Proust, Pirandello, Kafka, Robert Graves, Somerset Maugham (that virtuoso of detachment), Thomas Mann, Will Rogers ("Half our life is spent trying to find something to do with the time we have rushed through trying to save"), Billy Wilder (*Sunset Boulevard* is narrated by a *corpse*), Nabokov, Magritte, Brecht, E. M. Cioran (the Romanian aphorist was obsessed with the supreme irony of consciousness, that humankind's greatest achievement is also its greatest affliction), Evelyn Waugh, Groucho Marx (actually quite hostile), Camus, William Burroughs, Claes Oldenburg, Joseph Heller (*Catch-22* has entered the language as shorthand for absurd paradox), M. C. Escher, John Barth, Kurt Vonnegut, Philip Roth (only if you deem seriocomic-postmodern-experimentalist-metafictional-fiction ironic), Anne Sexton, George Carlin, Jack Nicholson ("My mother never saw the irony in calling me a son of a bitch"), François Truffaut, Umberto Eco (every word he writes means something else, including *and* and *the*), Calvin Trillin ("Math was my worst subject because I could never persuade the teacher that my answers were meant ironically"), Steve Martin, Paul Krassner (the motto of his underground paper, *The Realist,* was "Irreverence is our only sacred cow"), Andy Warhol (was he a master of irony or did irony master him?), John Waters (the mustache alone!), Martin Mull (always funny but I never believe a word he says), Kurt Andersen, David Letterman (before 9/11), Andy Kaufman (the self-described "anti-humorist" never "broke the fourth wall"), Bill Murray (may not have a single unironic bone in his body), Joe Queenan, Jim Jarmusch, Garry Shandling ("I think there is a great irony in the fact that I had to decide whether I wanted to host a show—because I was offered those late-night shows—or whether I wanted to do a show about a guy who hosts a show"), Dennis Miller (master ironic allusionist), John Malkovich (claims he can't act unless the words contradict what the character feels), Quentin Tarantino, Jerry Seinfeld ("irony incarnate," per Jed Purdy), Larry David (plays a character just like him named Larry David), Kathy Griffin,

Stephin Merritt, David Foster Wallace (though he considers himself a "realist"), Dave Chappelle, Louis Theroux, Jon Stewart (in a deliciously ironic reversal, *The Daily Show*'s "fake news" anchor excoriated CNN *Crossfire* hosts Paul Begala and Tucker Carlson for not taking their jobs seriously), Stephen Colbert, and the following.

John Waters's ironic mustache
(Getty Images/Evan Agostini)

JANE AUSTEN (1775–1817)

Witty chronicler of middle-class manners and morals in eighteenth-century England whose narrators employ understatement and irony to instruct and uplift readers. Austenian irony is gentle and constructive, an irony of engagement. She ironizes because she *loves*, and wants to make things better. Witness two examples from *Pride and Prejudice:*

It is a truth universally acknowledged, that a single man in possession of a good fortune, must be in want of a wife.

Elizabeth's eyes were fixed on her with most painful sensations, and she watched her progress through the several stanzas with an impatience which was very ill rewarded at their close; for Mary, on receiving, amongst the thanks of the table, the hint of a hope that she might be prevailed on to favour them again, after the pause of half a minute began another. Mary's powers were by no means fitted for such a display; her voice was weak, and her manner affected. Elizabeth was in agonies. She looked at Jane, to see how she bore it; but Jane was very composedly talking to Bingley. She looked at his two sisters, and saw them making signs of derision at each other, and at Darcy, who continued, however, imperturbably grave. She looked at her father to entreat his interference, lest Mary should be singing all night. He took the hint, and when Mary had finished her second song, said aloud, "That will do extremely well, child. You have delighted us long enough. Let the other young ladies have time to exhibit."

SANDRA BERNHARD (1955-)

Comedian-actress-singer known as the Queen of Irony for her satirical one-woman shows, she was a staunch defender of irony in the dark days immediately after 9/11:

> The minute you lose your sense of irony, you might as well blow your head off. What's the point of living if you can't see something deeper in every situation? That's what irony provides.
>
> —Sandra Bernhard, quoted by Neva Chonin in the *San Francisco Chronicle*, December 10, 2001

RANDOLPH BOURNE (1886-1918)

A progressive American social critic at the turn of the century, he employed irony as a weapon first against the militarism that swept the nation in 1915 and then against the subsequent world war, a stand that would isolate him for the rest of his short life (he died in the 1918 influenza epidemic). Bourne is probably best remembered for his unfinished essay, "War Is the Health of the State," a paean to the ironic life, which he defined as "a life keenly alert, keenly sensitive, reacting promptly with feelings of liking or dislike to each bit of experience, letting none of it pass without interpretation and assimilation, a life full and satisfying—indeed a rival of the religious life." The ironist is ironical, Bourne wrote, "not because he does not care, but because he cares too much."

SACHA BARON COHEN (1971–)

Cambridge-educated comedian whose *Da Ali G Show* is a cult favorite on HBO. "Ali G" is ostensibly a misogynistic malaprop of a black man from the London suburb of Staines (Baron Cohen describes him as an "overconfident ignoramus"), but the character is really a white man trying to be black: Ali G, it turns out, is not a Middle-Eastern name, but short for "Alistair Graham," a gangsta-rapper-wannabe send-up of middle-class kids who appropriate black street culture. Ali G, then, is a white man pretending to be a black man, which makes Baron Cohen a white man pretending to be a white man pretending to be a black man.

By telling guests they're appearing on an educational program for young people, the show's producers wangle interviews with such authority figures as Boutros Boutros-Ghali (Ali G introduces him as "Boutros Boutros Boutros-Ghali"), James Baker, Pat Buchanan, Newt Gingrich, C. Everett Koop, Ralph Nader, Brent Scowcroft, Richard Thornburgh, and former U.S. Attorney General Edwin Meese, who actually *raps* on the show ("I was attorney general / My name is Meese / I say go to college / Don't carry a piece").

Ali G is a twenty-first-century *eiron* who exposes pomposity by pretending to be stupid. He subverts stereotypes by reinforcing them. He asks cringingly embarrassing questions that his victims take seriously—or *pretend* to take seriously out of pathological political correctness—and thereby humiliate themselves, as did former National Security Advisor Brent Scowcroft and former Attorney General Richard Thornburgh:

Ali G:	Did they ever catch the people who sent Tampax through the post?
Scowcroft:	No, they did not. And it wasn't Tampax, it was anthrax.
Ali G:	I think they is different brand names. Like we say pavement, you say sidewalk, whatever. There is different words for the . . .
Scowcroft:	Well, maybe, but anthrax is the germ and Tampax is something very different.
Ali G:	What is legal?
Thornburgh:	Well, I think most conduct most of us engage in on a day-to-day basis is legal.
Ali G:	So, what is *illegal*?

Thornburgh:	What is illegal is what the elected representatives of the people define as crimes.
Ali G:	What is *barely* legal?
Thornburgh:	Well, that's where you get into technicalities and you have trials.
Ali G:	'Cause me saw dis film called *Barely Legal Three* and it was about these two naughty college girls and them have done their own work and then as punishment they had to have a three-header with their supervisor, this teacher. Is *that* to do with the law?
Thornburgh:	Uh, it's hard to say. That's probably governed by the rules of the institution, the college.

Bonus irony: The 2002 London premiere of Baron Cohen's feature film, *Ali G Indahouse,* was met with anti-racist protests, apparently on the ground that working-class black street culture is somehow exempt from parody, which, of course, is itself a racist attitude.

YOGI BERRA (LAWRENCE PETER BERRA, 1925–)

The former New York Yankees catcher and manager is celebrated as much for his unintentionally ironic pronouncements as for his accomplishments on the field:

We were overwhelming underdogs.

You can observe a lot just by watching.

When you come to a fork in the road, take it.

If people don't want to come to the ballpark, how are you going to stop them?

Bonus irony: One of Yogi's most famous lines, "I really didn't say everything I said," may not have been his: Over the years, sportswriters fabricated Yogi-esque quotes that Yogi adopted.

MASON COOLEY (1927–)

The American aphorist is both a practitioner and a connoisseur, as these selections from his *City Aphorisms* attest:

The ironies in the commonplace are my inspiration and delight.

A frog in love would not be enchanted to learn that her beloved had turned into Prince Charming.

Irony regards every simple truth as a challenge.

Self-pity makes people callous.

Irony dissolves sentiment, but occasionally a sentiment is strong enough to dissolve irony.

Travelers never think that *they* are the foreigners.

The moment of orgasm is no time for ironic comments.

DOUGLAS COUPLAND (1961–)

Post-ironic Canadian novelist, culture critic, and neologist who named "Generation X" and made it famous in his novel of the same name. Coupland's mordant coinages expose the vacuity of postmodern irony:

Knee-Jerk Irony: The tendency to make flippant, ironic comments as a reflexive matter of course in everyday conversation.

Derision Preemption: A life-style tactic; the refusal to go out on any sort of emotional limb so as to avoid mockery from peers. *Derision Preemption* is the main goal of *Knee-Jerk Irony.*

Obscurism: The practice of peppering daily life with obscure references (forgotten films, dead TV stars, unpopular books, defunct countries, etc.) as a subliminal means of showcasing both one's education and one's wish to disassociate from the world of mass culture.

O'Propriation: The inclusion of advertising, packaging, and entertainment jargon from earlier eras in everyday speech for ironic and/or comic effect: "Kathleen's Favorite Dead Celebrity party was tons o' fun" or "Dave really thinks of himself as a zany, nutty, wacky, and madcap guy, doesn't he?"

Squirming: Discomfort inflicted on young people by old people who see no irony in their gestures. "Karen died a thousand deaths as her father made a big show of tasting a recently manufactured bottle of wine before allowing it to be poured as the family sat in Steak Hut."

—**Douglas Coupland,** *Generation X: Tales for an Accelerated Culture* (1991)

JACQUES DERRIDA (1930–2004)

Algerian-born French philosopher and critic whose ironic "deconstruction" of literary and philosophical texts looks not at what is ostensibly intended but rather at the effect of what is stated, thus favoring interpretation over content.

> To pretend, I actually do the thing: I have therefore only pretended to pretend.
> —Jacques Derrida (attributed)

DAVE EGGERS (1970–)

Editor and founder of the literary magazine *McSweeney's* and author of *A Heartbreaking Work of Staggering Genius* (2000), a bestselling memoir of how he became the single parent of his eight-year-old brother after the deaths of their parents. Filled with self-consciously self-conscious reflections on self-reflection, *AHWSG* takes self-irony to sublimely ridiculous levels. Eggers, it turns out, is not only a practitioner and connoisseur, but also an irony-prescriptivist:

> When someone *kids around,* it does not necessarily mean that he or she is being *ironic.* That is, when one tells a joke, in any context, it can mean, simply, that *a joke is being told.* Jokes, thus, do not have to be *ironic* to be *jokes.* Further, *satire* is not inherently ironic. Nor is *parody.* Or any kind of *comedy.* Irony is a very specific and not all that interesting thing, and to use the word/concept to blanket half of all contemporary

cultural production—which some aged arbiters seem to be doing (particularly with regard to work made by those under a certain age)—is akin to the too-common citing of the "Midwest" as the regional impediment to all national social progress (when we all know the "Midwest" is ten miles outside of any city). In other words, irony should be considered a very particular and recognizable thing, as defined above, and thus, to refer to everything *odd, coincidental, eerie, absurd,* or *strangely funny* as *ironic* is, frankly, an abomination upon the Lord. (Re that last clause, not irony, but a simple, wholesome, American-born *exaggeration*).

—Dave Eggers, *A Heartbreaking Work of Staggering Genius* (2001 Vintage edition)

ALAN GREENSPAN (1926–)

More a master of obfuscation than irony, the former Federal Reserve board chairman warrants inclusion on this list for his impenetrable pronouncements, including the tour de force:

I guess I should warn you: If I turn out to be particularly clear, you've probably misunderstood what I've said.

—Alan Greenspan, speech to the Economic Club of New York, 1988

CHRISTOPHER GUEST (1948–)

Probably the world's foremost "mockumentarian," he wrote, directed, and acted in such quasi-improvisational classics as *Waiting for Guffman* (1996), *Best in Show* (2000), and *A Mighty Wind* (2003), but is perhaps still best known for his portrayal of Nigel Tufnel in the mock rockumentary *This Is Spinal Tap* (1984, directed by Rob Reiner).

JERZY KOSINSKI (1933–1991)

Polish-born American novelist whose suicide note read: "I am going to put myself to sleep now for a bit longer than usual. Call the time Eternity." Chance, the protagonist of Kosinski's 1971 novel *Being There,* is a simple-minded gardener who never left the estate until his employer died. His naïve, TV-informed utterances are mistaken for profundity by self-deluded stuffed shirts whose plans and schemes are thereby exposed as folly.

WILLIAM SHAKESPEARE (1564–1616)

The great English playwright and poet is the ultimate master of irony. His plays are all about the unintended consequences of words and actions; his characters are always making blunders caused by the gap between appearance and reality. Disguises, mistaken identities, and misunderstandings produce multiple layers of irony: Lear rejects the daughter who loves him most; Mark Antony's praise for Brutus is really blame; Olivia falls in love with her ideal man, who turns out to be a woman. And then there's Hamlet: ambivalent, alienated, solipsistic, and tragically ironic:

> There is nothing either good or bad, but thinking makes it so.
> —Hamlet, Act II, scene ii

> Irony is what keeps Hamlet going . . . he's the Dave Eggers of medieval Denmark.
> —Charles McGrath, "No Kidding: Does Irony Illuminate or Corrupt?", The New York Times, August 5, 2000

SARAH SILVERMAN (1970–)

Standup comic, actress, and writer whose irony springs from the incongruity between her demure persona and the scathing content of her material. Her punch lines are razor-sharp ironic twists:

> I was raped by a doctor. Which is so bittersweet for a Jewish girl.

> Everybody blames the Jews for killing Christ, and then the Jews try to pass it off on the Romans. I'm one of the few people that believe it was the blacks.

I was licking jelly off of my boyfriend's penis and all of a sudden . . . all of a sudden it hit me . . . Oh my God! I'm turning into my mother!

[The events of September 11] were devastating. They were beyond devastating. I don't want to say especially for these people, or especially for *these* people, but especially for *me*, because it happened to be the same exact day that I found out that the soy chai latte was, like, *nine hundred* calories. I had been drinking them *every day.* You hear soy, you think healthy. And it's a lie. It was also the day we were attacked.

I want to get an abortion, but my boyfriend and I are having trouble conceiving.

Appearing on *Late Night with Conan O'Brien* in 2001, Silverman told a joke that used an ethnic slur ironically. She eventually responded to the backlash . . . with more irony:

I got in trouble for saying the word *Chink* on a talk show, a network talk show. It was in the context of a joke. Obviously. That'd be weird. That'd be a really bad career choice if it wasn't. But, nevertheless, the president of an Asian-American watchdog group out here in Los Angeles, his name is Guy Aoki, and he was up in arms about it and he put my name in the papers calling me a racist, and it hurt. As a Jew—as a member of the Jewish community—I was really concerned that we were losing control of the media. Right? What kind of a world do we live in where a totally cute white girl can't say "Chink" on network television? It's like the fifties. It's scary. . . . There are only two Asian people that I know that I have any problem with, at all. One is, uh, Guy Aoki. The other is my friend Steve, who actually went pee-pee in my Coke. He's all, "Me Chinese, me play joke." Uh, if you have to explain it, Steve, it's not funny.

   —Sarah Silverman, quoted by Dana Goodyear, "Quiet
      Depravity: The Demure Outrages of a Standup Comic," *The
      New Yorker*, October 24, 2005

Silverman's deadpan contribution to *The Aristocrats* (2005), a documentary by Penn Jillette and Paul Provenza in which a succession of comedians tell their versions of a prototypical dirty joke, is the most inventive, and ironic, of the film:

Joe Franklin loved the Aristocrats. He was, like, our rehearsal director when Dad and my brother weren't there. And my mother, and my nana—weren't there. I was on his show. He said it wasn't a "taped show," but we, like, did a show. . . . It was his office, but he had a bed in it, like a couch, that he called Uncle Joe's bed for little people. Joe Franklin raped me.

According to Provenza, "If the choice of who raped her was anybody but Joe Franklin, we couldn't deal with it. But by making it Joe Franklin she spins it off into absurdity yet again. Imagine Joe Franklin being sexual. There's an irony in that alone."

JONATHAN SWIFT (1667–1745)

Poet, novelist, essayist, preacher, and one of the great satirists in the English language, his *A Modest Proposal* (1729) is a striking demonstration of the power of irony. Published three years after his masterpiece, *Gulliver's Travels,* its full title is: "A Modest Proposal for Preventing the Children of the Poor People in Ireland from Being a Burden to Their Parents or Country, and for Making Them Beneficial to Their Public." It calls attention to the exploitation of the Irish masses by their English landlords by dryly proposing that poor Irish parents earn money by selling their babies to the English as food, which will also help reduce overpopulation. The phrase "a modest proposal" has been used ironically ever since.

I have been assured by a very knowing American of my acquaintance in London, that a young healthy child, well nursed, is at a year old, a most delicious, nourishing, and wholesome food, whether stewed, roasted, baked, or boiled; and I make no doubt that it will equally serve in a fricassee, or a ragout.

As to our City of *Dublin,* Shambles may be appointed for this purpose, in the most convenient parts of it, and

Butchers we may be assured will not be wanting, although
I rather recommend buying the Children alive, and
dressing them hot from the Knife, as we do *roasting pigs*.

MARK TWAIN (SAMUEL LANGHORNE CLEMENS, 1835–1910)

American author who drew on his childhood along the Mississippi River to create masterpieces of realism, wit, and irony,
including *The Adventures of Tom Sawyer* (1876) and *The Adventures
of Huckleberry Finn* (1884), widely considered the best American novel.

Huck smokes and swears too much, but he's intelligent and
resourceful. His innate sense of justice leads him to help his
slave friend Jim escape from his "rightful" owner. It is ironic
that Huck brands himself a sinner for defying the morality that
deems anyone who "steals" a slave from his owner a bad person. With deadpan earnestness, Huck is the quintessential "unreliable narrator" who naïvely recounts adventures while
floating down the Mississippi on a raft, allowing Twain to make
sharp comment on human nature.

Bonus irony: *The Adventures of Huckleberry Finn,* one of the
great egalitarian statements in American literature, is still sup-
pressed as racist by school boards that fail to grasp its central
irony, that is, that Jim is the only honorable adult character in a
novel peopled by white murderers, liars, and hypocrites.

Against Irony

Irony tyrannizes us. The reason why our pervasive cultural irony is at once so powerful and so unsatisfying is that an ironist is impossible to pin down. All U.S. irony is based on an implicit "I don't really mean what I'm saying." So what does irony as a cultural norm mean to say? That it's impossible to mean what you say? That maybe it's too bad it's impossible, but wake up and smell the coffee already? Most likely, I think, today's irony ends up saying: "How totally banal of you to ask what I really mean." Anyone with the heretical gall to ask an ironist what he actually stands for ends up looking like an hysteric or a prig. And herein lies the oppressiveness of institutionalized irony, the too-successful rebel: The ability to interdict the question without attending to its subject is, when exercised, tyranny. It is the new junta, using the very tool that exposed its enemy to insulate itself.

—David Foster Wallace, "E Unibus Pluram: Television and U.S. Fiction," in *A Supposedly Fun Thing I'll Never Do Again* (1998)

Irony is spent as a cultural force. Around the time of
Lenny Bruce, the ironic posture was a thrilling *épater le
bourgeois* against repression, conformity, official
smugness, and fatuity. Now that the edifices have been
torn down, the ironic posture has itself become party to
the forces of official smugness and fatuity.

>   —Michael Hirschorn, *Slate,* September 22, 1999

Irony has only emergency use. Carried over time, it is
the voice of the trapped who have come to enjoy their
cage.

>   —Lewis Hyde, "Alcohol and Poetry: John Berryman and the
>   Booze Talking" (1975)

Irony is unrelieved vertigo, dizziness to the point of
madness.

>   —Paul de Man, "The Rhetoric of Temporality" in *Blindness
>   and Insight: Essays in the Rhetoric of Contemporary
>   Criticism,* second edition (1983)

I'm not interested in the irony of my position. Cancer
cures you of irony. Perhaps my irony was all in my
prostate.

>   —Anatole Broyard, *Intoxicated by My Illness and Other
>   Writings on Life and Death* (1992)

I know idealism is not playing on the radio right now,
you don't see it on TV, irony is on heavy rotation, the

knowingness, the smirk, the tired joke. I've tried them all out but I'll tell you this, outside this campus—and even inside it—idealism is under siege beset by materialism, narcissism, and all the other isms of indifference. Baggism, Shaggism. Raggism. Notism, graduationism, chismism, I don't know. Where's John Lennon when you need him?

—Bono, commencement address at the University of
Pennsylvania, May 17, 2004

More disheartening is the beating *The Phantom Menace* took for its earnestness. Each year, Hollywood's products grow more cynical and self-aware. If a movie eschews this oh-so-hip edge—if its young hero says his dream is to fly in a spaceship, and he means nothing more than that—then it will be mercilessly punctured by reviewers' barbs. In an age drenched with irony, sincerity is often rejected out of hand.

—Eric Larsen, the American Enterprise Online

Pleasure in irony . . . is an ego trip.

—Jessamyn West, *The Life I Really Lived* (1979)

Irony was a kind of autopilot, a default setting. It was what lots of academics and others thought "smart" meant, but it was tiresome and so many were fond of it. They were so disheartening. Why weren't they better?

—Frederick and Steven Barthelme, *Double Down:
Reflections on Gambling and Loss* (1999)

> When [irony] is not employed as an honest device of
> classical rhetoric, the purpose of which no healthy mind
> can doubt for a moment, it becomes a source of
> depravity, a barrier to civilization, a squalid flirtation with
> inertia, nihilism, and vice.
>
> —Thomas Mann, *The Magic Mountain* (1924)

Irony is appropriate only as a pedagogical tool, used by
a teacher interacting with pupils of whatever sort; its
purpose is humiliation, shame, but the salubrious kind
that awakens good intentions and bids us offer, as to a
doctor, honor and gratitude to the one who treated us
so. The ironic man pretends to be ignorant, and, in fact,
does it so well that the pupils conversing with him are
fooled and become bold in their conviction about their
better knowledge, exposing themselves in all kinds of
ways; they lose caution and reveal themselves as they
are—until the rays of the torch that they held up to their
teacher's face are suddenly reflected back on them,
humiliating them. Where there is no relation as between
teacher and pupil, irony is impolite, a base emotion. All
ironic writers are counting on that silly category of men
who want to feel, along with the author, superior to all
other men, and regard the author as the spokesman for
their arrogance. Incidentally, the habit of irony, like that
of sarcasm, ruins the character; eventually it lends the
quality of a gloating superiority; finally, one is like a

snapping dog, who, besides biting, has also learned to
laugh.

   —Friedrich Wilhelm Nietzsche, *Human, All Too Human*
    (1878)

I don't think there's been a single pun on any of my records for ten years and yet I'm known for that because of
the first few albums. And the same with irony—it's an
overplayed hand and it's also a juvenile hand. The
deliberate seeking of darkness and the sardonic, and
the denial of feeling and the denial of trust and belief,
it's something that you do when you're younger and it's
something that is right—part of it's genuine and part of
it is insecurity. I'm not saying that was all wrong. I love a
lot of the songs I wrote then, I still sing them, but there's
room in the world for lots of different points of view, lots
of different types of expression, even inside the
repertoire of one songwriter and singer.

   —Elvis Costello, quoted by Simon Hattenstone, *The*
    Guardian, August 30, 2003

Irony is a refuge for the insecure. We retreat into our
irony cages when we feel threatened by our difference
from other people. Finding out that you're not like
everybody else is hard. Yet the hurt that accompanies
this revelation decreases if that revelation stays private.
So long as we do not see other people seeing us as

"different" we can sustain the semblance of belonging. When I reveal my tastes under the sign of irony, I leave open the possibility that I'm not being serious, that I'm only pretending to have those tastes. If I sense that the people I'm talking to will accept my fondness for Wilco, World War II movies, or cheese soup, then I can gradually make it clear that I'm making a serious declaration of taste. On the other hand, if I don't sense that their acceptance is forthcoming, I can move on to another topic, knowing that I have, strictly speaking, told the truth. From this perspective, irony functions like those escape routes that governments devise for their leaders. It gives you an "out," but only when you need it.

—Charlie Bertsch, "The Spirit of Irony," *Bad Subjects,*
    posted in October 2000 at bad.eserver.org

There's terrific merit in having no sense of humor, no sense of irony, practically no sense of anything at all. If you're born with these so-called defects, you have a very good chance of getting to the top.

—Peter Cook, quoted by Ronald Bergan in *Beyond the Fringe . . . and Beyond* (1989)

In Defense of Irony

We cannot use language maturely until we are
spontaneously at home in irony.
   —**Kenneth Burke**, *A Rhetoric of Motives* (1950)

Irony is a disciplinarian feared only by those who do not
know it, but cherished by those who do. He who does
not understand irony and has no ear for its whispering
lacks eo ipso what might be called the absolute beginning
of the personal life.
   —**Søren Kierkegaard**, *The Concept of Irony* (1841)

Humor brings insight and tolerance. Irony brings a
deeper and less friendly understanding.
   —**Agnes Repplier**, *In Pursuit of Laughter* (1936)

A taste for irony has kept more hearts from breaking than a sense of humor for it takes irony to appreciate the joke which is on oneself.

—Jessamyn West, *The Life I Really Lived* (1979)

Objection, evasion, distrust, and irony are signs of health. Everything absolute belongs to pathology.

—Friedrich Wilhelm Nietzsche, *Beyond Good and Evil* (1886)

The armor of irony is a little ugly, it's difficult to lug around, and it makes it hard to hug one another. But maybe irony is, in the end, better than abs of steel.

—Veronica Rueckert, "The Post Modern Ironic Wink," *To the Best of Our Knowledge,* Wisconsin Public Radio, June 26, 2005

We live in a society heavily invested in predictable outcomes, risk management, plans for every contingency, and elimination of the unexpected. We are, in other words, into control, or at least the illusion of control. Irony invites us to step down from our pedestals, to loosen our anxious grip on life, to take ourselves a little less seriously, and to be healed. My guess is that being human has less to do with being in control than it does with rising to the various occasions that life hands us.

—Anthony B. Robinson, "Post-Election Musings on the Healing Power of Irony," *Seattle Post-Intelligencer,* November 13, 1998

Irony has more resonance than reason.

—Robert Lanham, *The Hipster Handbook* (2003)

Irony . . . has a long and honorable history as a rhetorical device. It isn't, as its critics are taking this opportunity to claim, the nihilistic acceptance of the worst of human nature, the universal "Whatever." More often, it's a rational response to consumer culture; all but the most credulous of us, once exposed to advertising, are budding ironists. And not so coincidentally, the ability to laugh at the difference between what we're told and what we experience means we have to recognize that difference—in other words, think critically. . . . An appreciation of irony doesn't preclude genuine emotion any more than appreciating baseball precludes liking football.

—Laurel Wellman, *San Francisco Chronicle,* September 25, 2001

Irony is the hygiene of the mind.

—Elizabeth Bibesco, *Haven* (1951)

There are no exact guidelines. There are probably no guidelines at all. The only thing I can recommend at this stage is a sense of humor, an ability to see things in their ridiculous and absurd dimensions, to laugh at others and at ourselves, a sense of irony regarding everything that calls out for parody in this world. In other words, I can only recommend perspective and distance.

—Václav Havel, address upon receiving the Open Society
Prize awarded by Central European University (1999)

Irony is not *for* anything. It has no higher purpose. It is a perspective on the world, one that takes advantage of distance and some weirdly skewed point of view to see everyday things—pomposity, convention, higher purposes, and the earnest advancement of points like this one—as ridiculous or sad or just somehow *other* than what they usually seem. It's a lens that is morally neutral, deployed for evil as easily as for good.

—Judith Shulevitz, *Slate*, January 4, 2000

America has a famously vexed relationship with its irony: Though our pop culture exports about 90 percent of the world's supply, the puritanical, isolationist, log-cabin region of the nation's oversoul prays nightly for its death. But in a world as complicatedly social as ours, it's not expendable—irony is social chess, the playful manipulation of lazy expectations. It's at least as important as love or sadness. Only total extermination of the species would kill it.

—Sam Anderson, *Slate*, November 10, 2005

It's easy to forget, in the wake of the various thudding political and cultural broadsides it's provoked, that irony ever had anything to do with subtlety. Most commentators and critics have comfortably equated the ironic mood with a smirking refusal to feel anything much beyond jaded pop-culture connoisseurship; matters have scarcely been helped by enterprising writers and filmmakers who have mined just that misapprehension in the cause of their own smirking, unfeeling minor celebrity.

But irony remains a supple, indispensable literary device, squaring comically misguided human desires and aspirations smartly against their messier worldly outcomes. Put another way, the antithesis of irony, the great idiom of unintended consequences, is not earnestness or sincerity, as is now so widely assumed, but tragedy—the blank hand of fate remorselessly stamping out consequences, blithely oblivious to our own puny intentions. Since it highlights the folly of our own longings against the indifference of the cosmos, irony is one of the only ways to register a feeble protest against this state of affairs while keeping something like a smile on one's face.

—Chris Lehmann, *The Washington Post*, March 26, 2002

Jesus wept; Voltaire smiled. From that divine tear and from that human smile is derived the grace of present civilization.

—Victor Hugo, *Oration on Voltaire* (1878)

Ironic, No?

Brewing heir Adolph Coors III was allergic to beer.

The "Marlboro Man" (actor David McLean) died of lung cancer.

Pima County (Tucson) Arizona supervisors held a closed meeting to discuss Arizona's open meetings law.

U.S. Border Patrol uniforms are manufactured in Mexico.

A Mexican national was arrested in 2003 for bringing two hundred pounds of marijuana into the United States concealed in the bumpers of his car, which he had purchased at a U.S. Marshal's auction in San Diego after it was used to smuggle illegal aliens and seized by the INS, which had failed to discover the hidden pot.

When the Berlin Wall fell in 1989, so many visitors were taking souvenir pieces that a protective fence was installed, so that, yes, the Berlin Wall was guarded by a wall. Bonus irony: Originally a barrier designed to keep East Berliners from escaping a Communist "worker's paradise," the Berlin Wall became a canvas for graffiti and other forms of ugly art that flourish in the West. The Berlin Wall thus went from a symbol of Soviet bankruptcy to one of Western decadence.

The Holocaust Memorial in Berlin is protected by an anti-graffiti veneer manufactured by Degussa, the same company that produced the chemical Zyklon B for Nazi gas chambers.

RKO's *The Conqueror* (1956) starring John Wayne as Genghis Khan was filmed in St. George, Utah, directly downwind from the Nevada atomic test site. By 1980, inordinate numbers of St. George residents and ninety members of the cast and crew had died of cancer, including director Dick Powell, costar Susan Hayward, and the super-patriot Wayne himself. In 1998, the state of Utah promoted St. George to tourists as "Utah's Hot Spot."

> I thought, Three nights ago I was up there bombing and now I'm down here [in a North Vietnamese prison] being bombed and I'm going to check out. Isn't that ironic!
>
> —John Yuill, American bomber pilot, on Operation Linebacker II, a massive bombing raid on Hanoi in 1972

Soon after San Francisco neurologist Dr. Richard Olney began conducting clinical trials to investigate the efficacy of cancer drugs on amyotrophic lateral sclerosis (and after spending decades caring for ALS patients), he was himself diagnosed with the disease and enrolled in his own study.

The author of a New Mexico state law mandating felony charges against owners of dangerous dogs was hospitalized after his own dog bit him on both arms.

I once talked to an old cannibal who, hearing of the Great War raging in Europe, was most curious to know how we Europeans managed to eat such huge quantities of human flesh. When I told him the Europeans did not eat their slain foes he looked at me with shocked horror and asked what sort of barbarians we were, to kill without any real object.

—Bronislaw Malinowski, *Argonauts of the Western Pacific* (1922)

In 1972, President Richard Nixon and White House chief of staff H. R. Haldeman discussed fellow Republican Ronald Reagan:

Nixon: Reagan is not one that wears well.

Haldeman: I know.

Nixon: On a personal basis, Rockefeller is a pretty nice guy. Reagan on a personal basis, is terrible. He just isn't pleasant to be around.

Haldeman: No, he isn't.

Nixon: Maybe he's different with others.

Haldeman: No.

Nixon: No, he's just an uncomfortable man to be around.

Later in the conversation, Nixon, one of the most peculiar men ever to have occupied the White House, actually describes the preternaturally affable Reagan as "strange." (Source: White House tape released in 2003.)

The Ronald Reagan Building, Washington's largest federal structure, is named after a president who said government was the problem and not the solution and promised to make it smaller.

One of the 1992 presidential candidates, H. Ross Perot, answered charges of mental instability by publicly dancing with his daughter to Patsy Cline's rendition of "Crazy."

H. Ross Perot
(AP Photo/Richard Drew)

Zimbabwe president Robert Mugabe's 2005 state of the nation address, in which he promised to remedy his country's chronic electricity shortages, was blacked out by a power failure.

Saddam Hussein spent almost a billion dollars on a series of impregnable underground bunker complexes, yet his last refuge was a five-by-eight-foot mud hole.

Jim Fixx, author of the bestselling *The Complete Book of Running* (1977), which popularized jogging as a means of life extension and helped start America's exercise revolution, died of a heart attack at age fifty-two while jogging. An autopsy revealed severely blocked coronary arteries.

Only six months ago, I discovered that, over the years, some cubby-hole editors at Ballantine Books, fearful of contaminating the young, had, bit by bit, censored some seventy-five separate sections from the novel. Students reading the novel which, after all, deals with the censorship and book-burning in the future, wrote to tell me of this exquisite irony. Judy-Lynn Del Rey, one of the new Ballantine editors, is having the entire book reset and republished this summer with all the damns and hells back in place.

—Ray Bradbury, *Fahrenheit 451* ("Coda," 1979)

The papers relating to Charles A. Lindbergh's 1927 transatlantic flight are stored in the Missouri Historical Society's library on Skinner Boulevard in St. Louis, the site of an old synagogue. Lindberg biographer A. Scott Berg noted the irony, given Lindberg's reputation as an anti-Semite.

In 1987 the Chicago Cubs traded relief pitcher Dickie

Noles to the Detroit Tigers for "a player to be named later." At the end of the season, the Tigers sent "the player to be named later" to the Cubs. It was Dickie Noles.

> The ironic philosopher reflects with a smile that Sir Walter Raleigh is more safely enshrined in the memory of mankind because he set his cloak for the Virgin Queen to walk on than because he carried the English name to undiscovered countries.
>
> —W. Somerset Maugham, *The Moon and Sixpence* (1919)

Stock car driver Edward Glenn "Fireball" Roberts (1931–1964) died in a fiery wreck during the World 600 in Charlotte, North Carolina, when his car burst into flames after hitting the inside wall. Bonus irony: Roberts's nickname derived not from his driving style but from his years as a hard-throwing sandlot pitcher.

During the filming of an episode of TV's *Homicide: Life on the Street,* a fleeing shoplifter blundered onto the set, saw the show's actors with their guns drawn, dropped the loot, and surrendered to them, thinking they were actual policemen. Bonus irony: In a subsequent episode, two homicide detectives encounter the crew of a TV show called *Homicide,* complete with Barry Levinson, who exclaims, "It's the real Homicide unit!"

In Frederica, Delaware, the suicide of a woman who hanged herself from a tree went unreported for hours because passersby thought the body was a Halloween decoration.

When a construction crew began repairing the decaying stone floor of the sculpture garden at Houston's Museum of Fine Arts, workers cordoned off an adjacent bas-relief with a red velvet rope and covered it in burlap. After a gust of wind loosened the covering and exposed a small portion of the sculpture, museumgoers were heard speculating on the artist's intent in providing only partial access to the work and about the symbolism of burlap juxtaposed with velvet.

Among the most damning evidence at Robert Blake's trial for the murder of his wife, Bonnie Lee Bakley, was testimony from bystanders who heard his frantic calls for help but didn't respond because, they said, he didn't sound "convincing," and from homicide detectives who claimed that when they informed Blake of his wife's death he put his head in his hands and wailed for thirty seconds, but no tears came out. Though Blake was acquitted by a jury that the Los Angeles District Attorney called "incredibly stupid," the actor was found liable at a subsequent civil trial for $30 million in damages. A juror said Blake "should have been more mellow" on the witness stand, and according to Duke Law School professor Erwin Chemerinsky, "Everything came down to the question: Is Robert Blake believable? Here the jury didn't believe him." Thus Blake lost the case as much for being a "bad actor" as for being a bad actor.

A seventeen-year-old Amish boy was electrocuted by a downed power line that tangled in the wheels of his horse-drawn buggy.

A United Parcel Service driver on his way to deliver parts to Cheshire Medical Center in Keene, New Hampshire, was involved in a serious accident. He was taken to Cheshire Medical Center by ambulance with a head injury, but the hospital could not perform necessary tests because one of its machines was down, and the parts to fix it were in the driver's wrecked van.

It's ironic that Joseph Pulitzer, owner of a newspaper known for sensationalistic reporting during his lifetime, has provided the eponym behind the most respected journalism award in the U.S. But there are other examples of whitewashing with the passage of time and the institution of awards. Alfred Nobel, who invented dynamite, is now better known for his Nobel Peace Prize. Who's to say one day we'll not have an annual Gates Prize for the company most admired for its fair business practices?

    —Anu Garg, A.Word.A.Day, posted on July 5, 2002, at wordsmith.org/awad

The publisher of *The Salt Lake Tribune* fired the company executive in charge of cost-cutting in what was described as a "cost-cutting" move.

Brad Pitt tore his Achilles tendon while playing Achilles in *Troy* (2004).

Sonny and Cher sang "I Got You Babe" on the David Letterman show at a time when they not only didn't *have* each other, they didn't even *like* each other.

Vincent Gardenia played the Bunkers' next-door neighbor on *All in the Family* twice: First as "Mr. Bowman," who sold his house to the Jeffersons, and again as "Frank Lorenzo," who bought the same house *from* the Jeffersons.

A 2001 Father's Day tribute on ESPN featured "How Sweet It Is (to be Loved by You)" sung by Marvin Gaye, who was shot and killed by his father in 1984.

Werner Klemperer (1920–2000), whose father, the conductor Otto Klemperer, had been forced to flee Germany in 1933 because he was half Jewish, won two Emmy Awards for his portrayal of Nazi Colonel Klink on the comedy series *Hogan's Heroes*.

In 1941, Deputy Führer of Germany Rudolf Hess, one of Adolf Hitler's closest advisors, flew solo to Scotland in hopes of negotiating peace terms with Great Britain. A letter Hess left for Hitler read in part: "If by chance, My Führer, this project, which I admit has but a very small chance of success, ends in failure and the fates decide against me, it will always be possible for you to deny all responsibility. Simply say I am crazy." Hess flew an ME-110 fighter obtained from his friend, aircraft designer Willy Messerschmitt, who did not know Hess's destination. Hess bailed out over Lanarkshire and was immediately taken prisoner by the British, a massive propaganda coup for the Allies. Meanwhile, back in the fatherland, an enraged Hitler issued a statement claiming that Hess was mentally ill and had undertaken the mission purely on his own initiative, then called Messerschmitt to account for releasing the plane to Hess. Pleading for his life, Messerschmitt asked,

"How was I to know that someone so high in the Reich could be crazy?"

> So ego, then, is the absence of true knowledge of who we really are, together with its result: a doomed clutching on, at all costs, to a cobbled together and makeshift image of ourselves, an inevitably chameleon charlatan self that keeps changing and has to, to keep alive the fiction of its existence. . . . Ego is then defined as incessant movements of grasping at a delusory notion of "I" and "mine," self and other, and all the concepts, ideas, desires, and activity that will sustain that false construction. . . . The fact that we need to grasp at all and go on and on grasping shows that in the depths of our being we know that the self does not inherently exist. . . . [The ego's greatest triumph] is to inveigle us into believing its best interests are our best interests, and even into identifying our very survival with its own. This is a savage irony, considering that ego and its grasping are at the root of all our suffering. Yet ego is so convincing, and we have been its dupe for so long, that the thought that we might ever become egoless terrifies us.
>
> —Sogyal Rinpoche, *The Tibetan Book of Living and Dying* (1993)

It is the male hormone testosterone that gives women their sex drive, not the female hormone estrogen.

One of the judges on the Massachusetts Supreme Court who ruled against gay marriage in 2003 is a lesbian.

Credit card companies refer to cardholders who pay off their outstanding balances every month, thereby avoiding finance charges, as "deadbeats."

Howard Hughes (1905–1976) had to die to prove he was alive: The "bashful billionaire" was so reclusive that for several years there was intense public speculation over whether he was dead or alive, and only after his body arrived in Houston, Texas, for an autopsy was it confirmed that he had actually been alive. Bonus irony: After lengthy probate proceedings involving various putative wills, most of the billionaire's fortune went to the Hughes Medical Institute, a charity Hughes had set up purely as a tax dodge.

> This is the first age that's ever paid much attention to the future, which is a little ironic since we may not have one.
> —Arthur C. Clarke (attributed)

The mid-nineteenth-century Arts and Crafts movement was a reaction to the extravagant ornamentation and mass production of the Industrial Revolution. Its founder, the English designer William Morris (1834–1896), wanted to return to simplicity and craftsmanship and create sturdy, comfortable, inexpensive furniture for common people. The famous Morris chair is the embodiment of that aesthetic. But the chair, fashioned in small shops with simple tools, was so painstakingly crafted, only the wealthy could afford it.

Morris chair
(Voorhees Craftsman, www.voorheescraftsman.com)

Bonus irony: Eventually the Arts and Crafts movement did create inexpensive, serviceable furniture for the great middle class, but only by means of the mass production Morris so abhorred.

Neural network or neural computing: computer architecture modeled upon the human brain's interconnected system of neurons, discerning and extracting the relationships that underlie the data with which it is presented. Most neural networks are software simulations run on conventional computers. . . . The network learns when examples (with known results) are presented to it; the weighting factors are adjusted— either through human intervention or by a programmed algorithm—to bring the final output closer to the known result.

Neural networks are good at providing very fast, very close approximations of the correct answer. . . . Among the tasks for which they are well suited are handwriting recognition, foreign language translation, process control, financial forecasting, medical data interpretation, artificial intelligence research, and parallel processing implementations of conventional processing tasks. In an ironic reversal, neural networks are being used to model disorders of the brain in an effort to discover better therapeutic strategies.

—Columbia Encyclopedia, Sixth Edition (2001–2005)

Entries for the Florida Press Club's 2005 Excellence in Journalism Award for hurricane coverage were lost in Hurricane Katrina.

In 2006, the Outdoor Life Network signed a deal to carry Arena Football League games.

High winds prevented workers from installing a wind data collection tower in Oneida, Illinois.

The rise of polio in the twentieth century resulted from improved sanitation. Discovery of the "germ theory of disease" in the nineteenth century led to higher standards of cleanliness, especially in technologically advanced Western Europe, Canada, and the United States. In less sanitary times, babies and very young children developed antibodies to poliomyelitis, a viral disease that causes paralysis, spinal damage, and even death. But a cleaner environment left increasing numbers of children with no natural immunity, so it was the industrialized countries—not those of the poorer, less developed "third world," that suffered the worst outbreaks of the disease.

A study by the National Science Foundation found that air purifiers using a process called "ionization" can generate ozone levels in a room that exceed the worst smog days in Los Angeles.

Americans are dumber than anyone realizes. Mike Judge's new movie, *Idiocracy*, about a future America where everyone is really stupid, has been dumped by Fox because test audiences didn't get the joke. Because they were too stupid to understand a movie about stupid people! Just when you think you've hit the bottom of the stupid barrel, you find out there's another barrel right underneath it.

—Bill Maher, *Real Time with Bill Maher*, September 15, 2006

A toothless man was arrested for stealing toothbrushes in Brazil. "I know it's a stupid thing to do," said the thief. "I have no teeth—what was I thinking?"

Are You Ironic?

Anthropologists have long tried to identify the one quality that distinguishes humans from other animals. Some believed it to be language, until Koko the lowland gorilla learned to sign in complete sentences. Some thought it was the ability to make and use tools, until a chimpanzee was observed using a straw to capture termites. Some have lately suggested that humans are the only species with self-consciousness. We may never know the answer, and this is just speculation, but what if it were our sense of *irony* that separates us from the rest of the animal kingdom? (At least some of us.) To be sure, the use and appreciation of irony can be important survival skills, and in order to develop those skills, it is useful to establish a baseline. Hence this test to measure innate irony. To compute your Irony Quotient, answer the questions, tally the numbers in parentheses, and refer to the chart at the end.

1. The following best describes my view of irony:
   A. Irony is a crutch. (0)
   B. Irony is okay, if you don't inhale. (2)
   C. Irony is the hygiene of the mind. (4)

2. How ironic am I?
   A. "Irony" is my middle name. (0)
   B. I'm somewhat ironic. (2)
   C. I'm not very ironic at all. Really. (4)

3. My most favorite expression is:
   A. Golly! (0)
   B. I could care less. (2)
   C. As it were. (4)

4. The following comes closest to my motto:
   A. Onward and upward! (0)
   B. Never say never. (2)
   C. Less is more. (4)

5. My response to irony in others is:
   A. Ironic people suck. (0)
   B. Ironic people are better than telemarketers.
      (2)
   C. Ironic people are the last hope for the
      human race. (4)

6. When someone points out the "irony" of Lou
   Gehrig's dying from Lou Gehrig's disease, I:
   A. Nod in agreement. (0)
   B. Cringe at the misapprehension of irony. (2)
   C. Reach for a baseball bat. (4)

7. My most favorite talk show host is:
   A. Donny Deutsch (0)
   B. Tavis Smiley (2)
   C. David Letterman (4)

8. When I use the term "big ole" to describe
   something large I'm being.
   A. Descriptive (0)
   B. Just a little bit country (2)
   C. Ironic (4)

9. My most favorite political commentator is:
   A. Bill O'Reilly (0)
   B. Bill Kristol (2)
   C. Bill Maher (4)

10. "Air quotes" are:
    A. Nifty (0)
    B. Okay if used sparingly (2)
    C. Pathological (4)

(Continued)

11. My most favorite comedian is:
    A. Carrot Top (0)
    B. Ray Romano (2)
    C. Stephen Colbert (4)

12. When I hear the words "family values," I think of:
    A. Mom and Dad (0)
    B. *The Sopranos* (2)
    C. *The Simpsons* (4)

13. My most favorite social critic is:
    A. Snoop Dogg (0)
    B. Andy Rooney (2)
    C. Douglas Coupland (4)

14. When I hear "o-rama" I think:
    A. Sale! (0)
    B. How dreary the free market can be. (2)
    C. "Palooza!" (4)

15. My most favorite leading man is:
    A. Adam Sandler (0)
    B. Tom Hanks (2)
    C. John Malkovich (4)

16. When Brooke Shields and Katie Holmes, then
    fiancée of Tom Cruise, both delivered baby
    girls on the same day in the same Los Angeles
    hospital, Shields told TV's *Access Hollywood,*
    "You know, the irony is perfect." During a
    Today show interview the previous summer,
    Cruise had faulted Shields's use of
    antidepressants for postpartum depression
    after the birth of her first daughter, insisting
    that postpartum depression should be treated
    with exercise and vitamins rather than drugs.
    The incident is an example of:
    A. Irony (0)
    B. Coincidence (2)
    C. Publicity (4)

17. My dream destination is:
    A. Utah (0)
    B. Amsterdam (2)
    C. Key West (4)

18. My most favorite female pop singer is:
    A. Alanis Morissette (0)
    B. Sade (2)
    C. Norah Jones (4)

(Continued)

19. A Weimaraner in a dress is:
    A. Art (0)
    B. Commerce (2)
    C. Pseudo irony (4)

20. When Senator John McCain raised soft
    money to finance his campaign against soft
    money, it was:
    A. Ironic (0)
    B. Politics as usual (2)
    C. Flamboyantly hypocritical (4)

21. My most favorite magazine is:
    A. *Entertainment Weekly* (0)
    B. *Wired* (2)
    C. *Mad* (4)

22. My most favorite blog is:
    A. Clusty (0)
    B. The Smoking Gun (2)
    C. Boingboing (4)

23. Which of the following statements about television is closest to the truth?
    A. Television is good. (0)
    B. Television is the opiate of the masses. (2)
    C. Watching television ironically is better than watching unironically, but not as good as not watching at all. (4)

24. My most favorite TV interviewer is:
    A. Larry King (0)
    B. Charlie Rose (2)
    C. Stephen Colbert (4)

25. When someone sarcastically tells me to "Have a nice day," I reply:
    A. "Thank you." (0)
    B. "Don't tell me what kind of day to have." (2)
    C. "Same to *you*." (4)

26. The difference between irony and sarcasm is:
    A. Irony is a crude form of sarcasm. (0)
    B. Sarcasm is a crude form of irony. (2)
    C. I'd tell you if I thought you'd understand. (4)

(Continued)

RESULTS:

  1–10 : Check for a pulse

 11–20 : Terminally literal-minded

 21–40 : Irony deficient

 41–60 : Some hope, but don't hold your breath

 61–80 : Borderline wry

 81–90 : Irony monger

91–100 : Congratulations, you Master of Irony, you

INDEX